How to Get Your Business to Make a Profit Without You
Copyright © 2006 by Mark Boersma
All rights reserved

Cover design by Mike Catuara and John Webb

Published by: Life in Action Publishing Company
28 W. 531 Woodland Road, Suite 501
Warrenville, IL 60555

The views expressed or implied in this work do not necessarily reflect those of Life in Action Publishing Company. Ultimate design, content, and editorial accuracy of this work is the responsibility of the author.

Printing services provided by Lulu.com

Printed in the U.S.A.

OUTLINE FOR BOOK

Version 2.20

INTRODUCTION

"Man's mind, once stretched by a new idea, never regains its original dimension."
- Oliver Wendell Holmes

Stretching can be beneficial on many levels. As a rule, we feel better physically when we stretch our bodies. Emotionally we gain new insights that we might never have known because we stretch ourselves to see all the perspectives that others may have. Spiritually we enhance our faith as we see life situations work out because we were willing to stretch and trust. These are large concepts that are literally life-long desires for most people. We expect to spend a great deal of time learning how to stretch and accept new ways of enriching our lives. Isn't it reasonable to assume that we will also stretch in our careers? Can we be open to new ideas and methods to make the stretching more profitable? That is what this book is all about.

I have been in business for 20 years. Some of those years have been spent working for others. When I first left college, I thought that was a stretch because I had to mold my learning with the goals and plans of my employer. Obviously all of my three degrees in business couldn't have totally prepared me for the real world. Nothing beats real experience. Sometimes I felt as though the stretching was really over the top. After marriage to my college sweetheart and the start of our family, I quickly realized that providing for my family was a definite priority. Many of the individuals reading this book can identify with the feeling that the real world asks more of us on a daily basis than we often feel prepared to deliver. That is why I wrote this book. I wanted to share some of my most practical ways to help others in business. You may view this book and its ideas as a stretch, but I guarantee you that you will look at your own business in a new light and give you new ideas to make it work.

Frankly, it has taken years to develop these ideas and systems. I am sure that many of you feel as though you have spent more than enough years trying to make your business profitable. Why aren't the profits and feelings of personal fulfillment what you expected? Why do you find yourself so involved in every decision? Why does the typical forty-hour week seem laughable? Is it because you are spending so much more time on your business? These are honest questions that most business people struggle with on a daily basis. I have been in your situation, and I can identify with the pain of not reaping what you are trying so diligently to sow.

It is my hope that you will be open to the new ideas that are presented in this book. Perhaps you will read a chapter and think that the basic concept is really quite fundamental. Maybe you will think back to people in your life who have tried to send you the same message. Yet, you realize that now is the time to focus on your business and how it can make a profit without you. Some of you will be thinking that it isn't making much of a profit WITH YOU. That is why this book is invaluable to you. Your desire to stretch and become a better business person is why this book appeals to you. I am about to offer you ways to make your business thrive. Imagine a business that succeeds when you put the right systems in place. Be open to new ideas that can change the direction of your business.

I want to emphasize that this is not a quick-fix book. We didn't get where we're at overnight and it's not going to change overnight. You might even need to invest more hours in the short-term to build and implement the systems but in the long-term it will work and you will end up getting your business to make a profit without you.

Part I CLIENTS

Chapter 1 - VALUING: GIVE THE CLIENTS THE MOST FOR THEIR MONEY

"Honest men esteem and value nothing so much in the world as a real friend." -

Bidpai

A.   Anticipate client's needs

B.   Under-promise and over-deliver

C.   Follow through with phone calls

Have you been shopping lately? Isn't everyone offering you the same merchandise or service at prices you really can't quite believe? It is no wonder the average store or business really doesn't exert much extra effort to get your sale. They really don't have to. The merchandise is similar everywhere and the buying public will take what they see. However, are they really satisfied with the product? Not always. That is why our sales approach needs to stand out in a sea of mediocrity. Your clients really need to feel special.

Being catered to in the business world really shouldn't be such an unusual way to treat people. Clients deserve to feel as though their needs and wants are being met. It is so important to understand what is necessary to make your clients' life easier. Think about the ways you have developed close relationships with people. How did you gain their confidence and trust? You really have to sit back and listen! So often we take our agenda and force-feed it to our clients! This backfires every time.

There are two major types of businesses, business to consumer and business to business. Whatever your business is, I want this book to benefit you. When we refer to customer we refer to your direct customer. This could be a consumer or it could be a business customer. I will refer to the consumer or business customer as a customer and a referral source as another business which refers you business. You will obtain referrals from clients but professional referral sources can significantly increase the number of high quality leads and reduce the time it takes to close them.

ANTICIPATE YOUR CLIENT'S NEEDS

I would recommend three basic precepts that will help you break down the barriers and get the client on your side. Remember, you can't sell them anything if they don't think you have their best interest at heart. Take a moment and think back to the successful seller/client relationships you have had. What makes it work for you? I would venture to say that what appeals to you on the buying side will also appeal to the client you are trying to reach. People's basic wants and desires aren't really that different.

1. Literally ask them what they are looking for in working with a professional in your industry.

2. Find out up front what they think they can afford to pay to make this happen.

3. Take notes on their needs and prepare a plan to help them reach their goals.

What is the consumer looking for?

Number one in the list is probably the most difficult. That is why it has to come first in the presentation. I recommend in-person interviews as the ideal because you can learn so much from seeing your client face to face. This is an area where people's personalities really play a major role. You need to make getting to know your client your very first priority. You will have only a short amount of time to assess the clients' attitude as you approach them. Make every effort to put yourself in their situation. Be open to their comments and suggestions for improving your service. Since many of us are guilty of "planning the attack" as we listen to others' hopes and desires, we miss so much. This can be deadly. The person on the other side of the desk can read you, and your sincerity counts.

Think about this role-playing exercise and see how it applies to your desire to reach your clients:

Salesperson: Thanks for coming to my office today. I really appreciate your time. What would you say are your top three goals in working with a (insert your industry here) professional?

Customer: I'm looking for excellent service, great prices/rates, and a very simple process that doesn't require much of my time.

Salesperson: Great! I want to make sure I have assessed all the areas you need help with. Are there any others?

Customer: Well, this whole process is pretty new to me. I think I may need some additional help to make sure I'm choosing the product/service that will be the best fit for me and my family in the long run.

Salesperson: I understand. I think you'll really enjoy seeing how our products/services are developed to meet your individual needs. Based on what you've said, I have a much better idea of what you need now.

This hypothetical scenario gives all parties a chance to express themselves. It is really a great fact-finding mission for the salesperson. Also, the customers feel as though the sales professional has taken the time to listen to them and understand their needs. It is not an attempt to shovel products and services into their lives, but rather an approach to meet individual needs.

Most importantly, the emphasis should be on the ways you and your company can assist the client in the buying process (how they can spend less time and money, how to make the process smooth and easy, etc.). People are receptive to a common-sense approach to solving their problems.

Find out what they can afford to pay

It is wise to put the cards on the table when it comes to finances and the costs for your client. This is good business for the customer as well as the salesperson. Seeing the person face to face can make a huge difference in what you choose to offer. People tend to be more honest about their financial picture when speaking directly to you. Also, you can see exactly what kind of business they are operating. This makes your evaluation so much more beneficial – for you and the client.

This is also why doing your homework pays off. If you are very familiar with your systems/products/services and how they help others, you can be mentally prepared to offer the client the best product(s) for their needs. While you definitely need to be well scripted for any situation, don't plan on using a prepared script to get you through your first in-person meeting with a client. You should instead put yourself in their position. What do they need and what can they afford?

Take notes and begin preparing a method to help your client

I have found that it really helps to take notes while the customer is talking. Conversations can get diverted quickly, so it is wise to get the main points that the client is discussing. Also, these notes can be helpful when you return to your office to fine-tune what you offer your client. Don't misquote the customer. By taking notes, you can accurately review the exact things the customer requested. It is common to think we have represented the customer when we have really only gathered information that is too general to assist them. Each client has specific needs and wants!

While you are jotting down the client's desires, you can begin formulating a plan to accomplish the goals for the customer. Again, put your focus on listening to what the client needs and can afford; however, certain key systems/products/services you are familiar with will come to mind as clients speak. Give the client a full opportunity to explain his situation and make sure that you aren't rushing the fact-finding phase. Think about the times you have waited and waited to see a doctor. Once the doctor appears, do you feel as though you have to rush because the poor guy next door has been waiting forever, too? Obviously you won't get all of your questions answered if you feel you need to hurry. It is imperative that you put the client at ease. Imagine how much easier it will be to develop a system, product, or service process for someone when you have really taken the time to get to know the client's desires.

UNDER-PROMISE AND OVER-DELIVER

Once the listening phase is over, you have the golden opportunity to tell your client why the products/services you offer will make such a huge difference in his or her life. Be assured that while the client was relating her needs, she was watching you to see how you reacted to those points. Clients will value the fact that you have given your time to listen and be attentive. Now it is time to show them why your systems stand out from the rest. Now is the time to be honest and sincere as you zero in on their needs.

In some ways this heading seems contradictory. Why would a good salesperson under-promise on his systems, products, or services? I like to think of this as taking the high road to honesty and sincerity. So many times as ordinary consumers we are given a "line" about the goods we purchase. The advantages of the product are really too unbelievable to imagine. It reminds me of the saying, "If it seems too good to be true, it is!" However, as we listen to a presentation, we somehow want this product to be able to cure all the ills we are suffering. Thank heaven someone has come along with the panacea that will save us from destruction! Deep in our heart we are skeptical, but the offer seems so great. The idea of taking a cure-all diet pill comes to mind. Forget about all the exercise and eating right. Well, let's be realistic. Few cures are that easy!

The systems, products, or services you offer are probably meant to be customized. This comes from allowing the customer to relate his or her real needs. Being honest about the time it will take to see a difference between their current situation and their new situation as they begin working with you is very important. Never fall into the habit of giving the customer false hopes about what is required to accomplish his goals. I realize that there is a fine line between honesty and brutal truth. You have to walk that line. Don't underestimate the customer's intelligence. They are fully aware of the fact that they really can't get something for nothing. Be encouraging without being evasive. Tell it like it is!

In my years of experience, the good times are about to begin after the customer is realistically given the advantages of the systems, products, or services he or she has chosen. Now, as the salesperson, you can take the ball and literally run down the field with no obstructions. You are free to OVER-DELIVER. How is that accomplished? Once you have been given the permission to put the systems in place, you also have the freedom to give the client the WOW experiences that can come with what you offer.

You are putting a program together that will literally exceed the expectations of your customer.

Follow through with phone calls

Communication is the key to making all the promises come through for your customer. It is time to initiate the products and services that can literally take the effort out of your customer's business. Your sole purpose is to make his life easier and more profitable. That has to be accomplished by setting up a phone call system and/or an e-mail system that enables you to return calls or e-mails within 24 hours. You have to approach this from the perspective of a consumer who wants to be notified immediately about his purchase. Your systems are effective because they have quick turn-over time. The client hears from your company within a very short period of time. I have found that the most effective way to reach out to consumers is via a phone call or e-mail. Obviously, these methods need to be short and concise so that the interested parties can get the information they need quickly. That is the beauty of your systems. They are customized for your customer's industry. Your job is to make sure that the systems go out consistently and efficiently to the interested people.

Have you ever set up an appointment with a person in the trades to fix something in your home? You really need their expertise because the broken item is not something you want to fix. Typically you get the promise – "I'll be calling you very soon to set up a time to fix your problem." What does that mean to you? I feel that I am a person who has built my business on the premise that "very soon" means within 24 hours. How many of you have waited days or weeks to hear back from that repair man? Your needs are still there, but the "fix" is far away. This is why the systems that you have customized for your client need to be totally ready to go. You will definitely want their approval to send the phone messages and e-mails out to their prospects, but this has to be in place once you know the client's needs. Don't lose sight of the goal – make the customer's life easier and more profitable without him or her getting overly involved. You have to become their most prized assistant in the pursuit of reaching others.

Here's a working example of how this plays out in the business world:

Salesperson: I am ready to get the ball rolling with the systems we have agreed on. I've been up-front with you about the fact that it will take some time to penetrate the prospects with your message. However, I want you to know that the systems will be consistently sent out to your prospects with your approval. Your message will be repeatedly on the minds of other business professionals. And the really good news is that we do this for you! These customized systems send out your message.

Customer: That is great. You mean that I don't have to draft or rewrite the text that goes out to my prospects? I thought I might have to do that.

Salesperson: No. The systems will start as soon as you give us the go-ahead. We have done so much research on these, and we know the turn-around time for them to penetrate the prospects so that you can get results. It is a process. As we discussed in the beginning, don't expect results in the first week. We were honest with you. However, by staying the course, you will see results.

It is fair to say that in the beginning you will have to reassure the client. This reminds me of my first jobs and the initial stages of working at a new place. Would I ever learn the format the company was promoting? Would I ever be able to act on my own without checking with another employee? Would I ever feel confident and content in knowing that I am doing the work well? All those questions come to mind, and they haunted me for a while. However, as the salesperson you have to put the client at ease and assure them that the systems are tested and true. You have watched it happen for others, and you are about to watch it happen for that person. Think of yourself as a mentor who is trying to make this transition easy.

I want to give you an example of someone who took us up on the offer and changed his business dramatically. One of the great advantages to these customized systems is that they can literally go around the world. I have certainly been a part of watching a professional's business expand because the systems went into immediate action for the client.

This client really stands out in my mind because he was so enthusiastic and ready for suggestions to help his business. He is a fair-minded individual who looks at his business rationally. I had to approach "valuing" this man in a sensible and profit-oriented way. In my estimation, this is what makes giving your client value so satisfying. It is essential to focus in on their most pressing need and meet that need. In this case, I saw his sales-closing numbers and felt that this was the area to hit on to bring him the most value. Obviously, the focal point with each client may vary, but the systems you have put in place before the interview will lend themselves to customizing. My client was ready to boost that sales-closing ratio. Now I could start fulfilling those promises and following through with thorough communication to make his business more efficient.

We began with systems that evaluated his income goals. Also, I needed to calculate his sales-closing ratio from previous years. With that information at hand, I could start developing the trust needed to convince my client that I had the tools to help him increase that ratio and enhance his profitability. This man wanted results, and it was my job to deliver.

One of my Michigan clients (Phil French) was given value through our e-mail systems. He expressed a desire to reach his many clients more efficiently. We had systems in place to put those e-mails out and reach his database with his message and business opportunities. What made the difference for this client was the swiftness of the operation. Again, I can't stress enough the importance of having systems ready to go into action for your client. This man felt we delivered for him because the product was ready to roll.

Another client expressed the same kudos regarding our systems. He felt that his time was valuable and was so relieved to deal with people who had systems in place to help him. Most business people don't have the time to create their own systems from scratch. When they are asked to relate their business plan, they often stop cold. What a joy to deal with a caring and organized company who has tested out systems that are ready to roll. This particular client was told that if he implemented these tools 90% of the time, he would see 94% results! Not a bad percentage, to say the least. It was really a no-brainer. The simplicity of the system amazed him, and the end results were worth the effort.

Amy Bendigkeit: Amy is a great example of how a sales professional/business owner is always ready to do business. Amy is always looking for opportunities to expand her business and assist those partners around her grow their business as well. Amy knows that as her partners around her grow their business she will also see her business grow too. She creates a WIN WIN WIN for everyone she works with.

Ready to talk real estate:

Amy Bendigkeit will talk real estate any time, any place. Ask her about new subdivisions while she's working out at her health club? No problem. Want to chat about market times while Bendikeit's doing her grocery shopping? No problem.

Bendigkeit, a Realtor ® with Glen Ellyn office at Koenig & Strey Real Estate, not only doesn't mind discussing the real estate at these moments, she looks forward to it. Why? This is because she always has an answer for every real-estate-related question.

"I study market listings before I go to cocktail parties," Bendigkeit said. "If you don't know about that new listing that's just come on the marketing, that's when people will ask you about it. Literally, I feel like I'm always on. I'll be at the health club pulling down weights, and people will want to talk to me about market times. But that's good. That means people recognize me and that they respect what I have to say. The moment the questions stop, I'll be quite sad."

Bendigkeit has worked in residential real estate for 13 years, and has never stopped educating herself about her market. Today, business is strong. Bendigkeit last year closed 26 million worth of real estate transactions.

Bendigkeit doesn't hesitate when asked why she's been so successful. She points to the moment about 10 years ago when a mortgage lender introduced her to Synergy Solutions, Inc. and their nationally known business coaching system. Intrigued, Bendigkeit tried out the system.

Synergy Solutions, Inc. encouraged Bendigkeit to create her own business plan and then work toward achieving the goals spelled out in it.

"You know your priorities when you go with a plan," Bendigkeit said. "When you know your priorities you can more efficiently work them."

Inspired by the coaching system, Bendigkeit decided that she needed to treat her business like a business. That meant building a staff. Today her staff includes a buyer's agent, administrative assistant, marketing coordinator, closing coordinator and even an assistant who helps Bendigkeit stage her listings to help them sell as quickly as possible. Synergy Solutions, Inc. also taught Bendigkeit how important it is to develop mutual referral sources. Bendigkeit will now only refer business to lender, accountants, lawyers and other professionals that also repay the favor and refer business back to her.

These tips have helped Bendigkeit steadily grow her business. Previously she sold about $7 million of real estate a year. Now, she sells more than three times that in an average year.

But numbers don't mean much to Bendigkeit. Instead, she focuses on her performance.

"Honestly, after all the dust settled from last year, when I sold more real estate than I ever had before, I decided that I would just keep on moving. That's the key. If you look sideways during a race, you lose. You have to keep looking forward and you have to keep moving. That's how I look at my business."

These stories emphasize the success side of having your act together so that you can meet the client's needs. However, how many of you have butted heads with individuals in business, and they just aren't as cooperative as the people I have just described? It is usually the case that we remember those people more clearly than the ones who jumped on board and said, "Bring on the value!" Many people seek help, but not all are willing to take the medicine that will put them on the road to financial health.

In general, I found the most difficult clients to be those who really wanted to hear a pat answer about their business. This isn't always evident from the onset. However, as you spend more time with them, you begin to realize that they are really not ready to implement new ideas. They are a lot like the overweight fellow who goes to the doctor and steps on the scale but has no intention of looking at the numbers. They tend to have reached the point in their business where they realize that the profits aren't matching the time expended, and they are even willing to listen to some solutions. The catch comes when the solutions don't match their preconceived conclusions. You are sincerely trying to bring value to them and set up systems that will make their business more efficient and profitable, but they aren't going to budge. This presents a real problem for you. How much time do you devote to a business that really doesn't want a cure?

Later in the book I will spend time on the personalities you tend to meet in business. Let's just agree at this point that it is almost impossible to set up a valuing scenario for a client who is bucking you all the way. Some people tend to think they want the value, but your systems somehow won't make them happy. It is counterproductive for you to keep trying to bring a plan to a client who really doesn't want to accept your suggestions. Yet, don't think this is totally the end of a relationship. I would recommend quarterly contacts with that client to assess their needs at that time. It is very possible that your solutions will look so much better as the year progresses. Remember, if it was important enough to pursue this client in the first place, it is important enough for you to keep in contact for a year. You are positioning yourself to be valuable to this client because you keep the promise of communicating with them. The systems are based on the premise that profits are reaped when we keep relationships thriving. Never discount perseverance!

The first stage to success for you and the client is setting up a *valuing* environment. Once that is established, you can proceed to the next phase. As in a good marriage, you are about to get to know your mate a lot better. Dr. Phil, Opera's favorite counselor, is right about many things, but he is definitely right about this: COMMUNICATION IS THE KEY. Now the journey gets into the area of finding out more about the client and his business. You have convinced them that you have their best interest at heart, and now they can open up and give you the opportunity to really make their business profitable.

TABLE ONE

Advantages of giving prompt value

1. You readily present systems that are established and dependable.

2. The client sees results in 30 days or less.

3. The client learns to trust you right away. Your word becomes fact.

Disadvantages of promised but delayed value

1. You keep searching for the "perfect" solution.

2. You keep promising results that may take months.

3. The client wants to trust you because of the cost and time investment.

Conclusion

The moral of the story is quite simple. People want value for their efforts and their money. Have you ever had a new furnace installed with the promise of a cheaper electric bill? Well, that bill had better deliver or the investment just wasn't worth it for you. People expect results for their investment. If you anticipate the client's needs, over-deliver on the promises, and follow up consistently with e-mails and phone calls, you will give the customer real value. This is the place to start!

Part II   REFERRAL SOURCES

Chapter 2 – Questioning

"No question is ever settled until it is settled right. Settle the question right." -Ella Wheeler Wilcox (1850 - 1919)

A.   Why it's important to earn $20,000-70,000 more

B.   Plant thought of 30 leads on first in-person contact

C.   What are the key questions to ask?

D.   How can they best be used?

Why it's important to earn $20,000 – 70,000 more

What if you could offer your business client an increase of $20,000 to $70,000 this year? Who wouldn't want to be the recipient of a salary boost like that? Many people are willing to accept a small increase of only two to three percent. Obviously you can't promise each business client a $20,000 to $70,000 increase in salary; however, it is wise to begin planting the idea that it is possible. Your client must begin thinking is terms of multiplying his business because of the systems you have already developed and honed. Conceiving of a company that can generate that kind of additional income is often just what the business client needs to contemplate. It is your goal to make this possible for your business client. The systems are designed to generate more income because of all the people they reach out to, and you are the facilitator. The numbers sound wonderful. Who wouldn't want an increase like that? Essentially, you are showing the business client the potential of putting the tools together to make it happen.

Professional referral sources are different from clients who refer you business as they are individuals who have businesses themselves, know a large group of people, or have access/influence to a large group of people who they can refer and influence to do business with you. Examples would be Realtors to loan officers, financial planners to accountants, insurance agents to Realtors, builders to financial planners, doctors to accountants, beauticians to dentists, and the list goes on and on. Every business can have professional referral sources but few do. The way to identify potential referral sources is to review the list of services/products your current clients use and then start to make a list of companies and individuals who you may be able to contact to better build your businesses together.

The six simple steps to do this are:

1. Identify the target
2. Develop the right message and deliver it
3. Ask key questions
4. Present solutions
5. Implement solutions – relationship starts to develop
6. Implement systems – solidify relationship and build businesses together

Now the process can begin as you explain the instrument that will allow your business client to literally reach out to 30 leads on the first in-person contact. This move is putting the business client into the driver's seat as he or she thinks about tapping into that many prospects. Your systems are driven by the promise that multiple contacts are not only possible; they are the norm. The business client has to begin thinking of his business that way – more income as a result of more viable contacts.

This is the segment of putting systems into place that really proves if you have done your homework well with your business client. It is imperative that you ask the business client the following pertinent questions to best serve his needs. After years of experience, I have found that these three questions really focus on the professional referral sources and/or business client needs and wants for their business. Fortunately they are not intimidating; however, they do help you to choose the best ways to really meet their needs and desires. As previously stated, if these are covered in the initial in-person interview with them, you have already formulated a plan to assist them.

QUESTION ONE:

How many hours are you working and how many would you like to work?

QUESTION TWO:

If you had ten leads with a lead being a name and a phone number how many of those would turn into a client? The average in most industries is one out of ten. How many would you do?

QUESTION THREE:

What is your WOW income goal? This would be your income that would make you feel incredible if you reached it.

Other great questions you can ask are: What is the biggest challenge you are facing in your career right now? What steps are you taking to ensure your businesses' long-term growth? Are there marketing systems in place? Are you thinking about hiring an assistant? Are you in a group that can bring you leads for your business?

Some people may view the third question as just an attention getter, but I have found otherwise. Years ago I heard a story about a student in a college class. The first few classes are fact-finding for both the teacher and the student. Each side is evaluating the other. In this particular class, the professor asked the students to write down the grade they thought they would be receiving at the end of the semester. Seems a bit unusual, doesn't it? The students have no idea what to expect from the teacher, and the teacher is really not familiar with the intellectual capacity of the students. How could a student have any idea about a final grade? Nevertheless, the students followed the instructions and put down the grade they "expected" to get at the end of the term. The professor collected the results from the students and kept them until the semester ended. Well, the oddest thing happened – the predicted grades matched the final grade in almost every case. Why? The professor said that the students know themselves and tend to work at that level. How interesting!

Is it true in real life, too? Yes! Business people tend to set an expected salary and stay near that level. They envision an income and feel that the amount is exactly what they are worth. The same numbers seem to keep coming up for them and the final income remains the same. By asking your client to put down a WOW income, you are forcing them to think outside the box. It's like visualizing themselves winning the Professional Businessperson of the Year Award. Does this seem like far-fetched wishful thinking? It wouldn't be wishful for the person who won the award. That person would feel as though they had earned it. We all have a little voice inside that says it's okay to work up to a certain level, but what if we dream of bigger returns? By encouraging your professional referral source or business client, you are heading him or her toward a worthy goal.

The other questions bring us all back to reality. What are your challenges? Everyone has them. It may be a challenge for your client to narrow it down to their biggest challenge. However, it is necessary to do that to focus on the area that needs the most immediate attention. Zero in on the biggest challenge and that is where you will see the results when the systems you provide start making that challenge manageable. Again, be a helpful interviewer and make sure your professional referral sources/ business client is truly being honest about the area that needs the most attention. As the questioning phase continues, I am reminded of Barbara Walters, a major TV personality. Doesn't she ask the best questions? She has practiced that technique, and you need to practice, too. The client can easily get distracted and begin telling you stories about all the woes they face daily. Bring them back to task and find out the biggest challenge.

As you approach the more personal or in-depth questions, you have to take a breath because you are about to tread into deeper waters. Everyone has a problem, but does everyone have a clue about a solution? Not always. By asking them about their company's long-term growth, you are sending them into the future. Many people are overwhelmed with today. This is where your people skills come into play. You don't want to scare them off, but you have to gently bring them to the realization that their business has to look forward to succeed. As their facilitator, you want to impress on them that the finished business is dependent on setting up concrete systems that keep on making their business profitable as time goes on.

Thorough marketing systems can really make a huge difference in a client's business. You are responsible for asking the referral source/clientif he or she has them already in place. Most will mention some occasional mailings or phone calls. People know that communication is important, but keeping that consistent is really difficult. Just keeping up with the daily chores of running their business can make scheduled marketing a problem. We all want to say that we service our prospects well, but the truth is often not that satisfying for either party. You need to be ready with a marketing system that will shock and awe your client. It will be a constant force in an ever-changing world. This is a positive thing!

Some of your professional referral sources/ business clients will tell you that not only is their job too demanding, but they really need to consider hiring an assistant to take part of the load. Haven't we all wanted a private secretary to

Handle all the mundane tasks? I remember the premise of the comedy film, "Multiplicity." Michael Keaton was so stressed as a married man with a family that he "cloned" himself to get some much-needed assistance. The movie is quite funny because the "clone" doesn't quite do his job the same way he would, and, naturally, his wife and kids don't know why they are suddenly confronted with another person who looks like their dad but doesn't really act exactly like him. It was a great idea and quite hysterical on the screen, but not always workable. Michael Keaton found out what we all find out: each person is very unique. Hiring an assistant is no guarantee that the work will be carried out exactly to our specifications. You need to offer the client a "clone" that is tailor-made to his or her business without the owner having to hire an actual person.

The systems aren't formulated to put individuals out of work. The beauty of these is that they work behind the scenes to bring the client's marketing information to the public without having to supervise a new employee. The program runs itself! Now the idea of making more money doesn't sound so far-fetched. There are people and systems in place to make it happen.

Another area to cover with the referral source/client involves a leads group, or an avenue to get new prospects on a regular basis. Once again, the ordinary demands of their business may keep them from meeting or contacting new people. This can mean total stagnation to their business. Conscientious people tend to think that keeping existing clients happy is their paramount goal; however, no new contacts will stop them dead in the water. This concept is often difficult to convey. How can I do a good job and service my clientele if I keep spending valuable time looking for new contacts? It is like asking a person to ride two bikes at the same time. Your ready-made tools will allow that person to keep those two bikes rolling along. You are offering them a program that does the communication for them. It takes the worry and concern out of the picture because the client can continue to feel satisfied that he or she is taking good care of the current customers while reaching out for new business.

Conclusion

All these questions are helpful. They give you a very good indication of your referral sources/ business client's business needs. In a relatively short amount of time you have focused on the main areas that need immediate attention. Now it is up to you to put these systems in place to meet those needs. To be honest, this is the critical part of the operation. Yourreferral source/clienthas agreed to let you question them and is counting on you to implement the right program. You have to be able to deliver with systems that will work best for this person and their business. Be ready, willing, and able to put the best program into place based on their answers to the questions. Staying focused now is the best course of action. They want to see results, and you are going to deliver.

Chapter 3 - Trusting

"Trust that man in nothing who has not a conscience in everything." - Laurence

Sterne (1730 - 1768)

A.   Added value

B.   Consistency

C.   Position yourself as a solution provider

As Dr. Phil would say, "How's that working for you?" How is the client feeling now that the relationship is on its way? The interesting thing about Dr. Phil's question is that it totally applies to both the people behind the efficient business tools and the client who is paying for them. A recent Harvard study underlines this precept in the medical world. This may not sound that revolutionary, but patients do better physically with doctors that they trust and enjoy a good relationship with. Wow! Did it take Harvard to bring that fact to light? Yet, think about that in the business context. The systems are in place now to meet the client's greatest needs; however, they will soon be nothing but good ideas if you don't develop that trust factor. Your client needs to know that his or her best interests are paramount. How do you accomplish that?

Bringing the client added value is a concrete way to show you truly care about maintaining their business. This needs to be more than just a promise to keep in touch. The client has to visibly see this added value as the relationship continues. The value items that have proven to be very successful are weekly e-mails, direct mail, client expectation questionnaires, lead tracking, free analysis tools, and other similar types of tools and systems which save your referral sources/business clients time and money. I will explain the development of that database in Chapter Four, but for now it is important to bring home the point that your client will realize results the fastest when you put the systems into place immediately. Your interview session has directed you to the best e-mails for your client. What a relief for them to know that those are totally ready to go!

Your systems are developed to be extremely consistent. The systems are set up as turnkey and are pre-approved by your referral sources/ business client. I have found that they are not only glad to see a system that is pre-planned for them, but they are very willing to get this moving because they are trusting me to show them results. I have been honest in telling them that it will take approximately three to six months to see direct results from many of these systems and tools, and they have accepted that reality. Fortunately my referral sources/ business clients have also been offered to help their referral sources/ business clients systems as well. It is a triangle of strength that can tie it all together for their business. I have been sensitive to their marketing budget, but I do offer this to make the results more effective. My goal: give them the most for their money and produce the quickest results. Take the work out of the picture for them! Here's an example of an e-mail that has proven to be affective in reaching out to clients. This would be considered an introductory e-mail to set the tone for others to come:

I thought you might appreciate a quick rundown of my goals in communicating with you. What I'm basically trying to do with these e-mails, postcards, and phone calls from my team is to bring huge benefit to your business and help you help it grow in any way I can. I don't want to overwhelm you, and I definitely want to give you info on the topics that are most relevant to you, *so any feedback you have would be much appreciated.*

If you'd like to hear a little more about me, how I do business, and some of the systems I've put in place that may help you increase your income and work fewer hours, my number's right by my name below!

This initial e-mail is friendly and non-invasive. Yet, it tells the referral sources/ business client's database that your client is trying to reach out to them in a positive way. It is meant to foster cooperation from business professionals who WANT to be a part of the communication process. The advantage to all of this is that it keeps your client's name in view while helping others with relevant topics about improving their own business. It is really a win-win! In my estimation, we can all greatly benefit from sharing business tips from others. Your systems are developed and relevant to today's business climate, and your personal client can reach out to others while helping them at the same time. This is really a unique opportunity for all parties.

The systems that have been "put in place" to help professionals increase their income and work fewer hours are concrete issues that all business people face. Your client becomes important to other professionals because he or she is offering them ways to better their situation. Here's another example

I do business a little differently than most professionals. I have learned the value of attention to the details of others' businesses in addition to my own. I desire to help you discover and improve areas where your business needs some attention. Then, in turn, perhaps you will give me the courtesy of referring some of that new business to me and considering a mutual referral partnership. I want to do whatever I can to help you in both your business and your personal life, because I care about every aspect of your life, not just the business I could potentially receive from you.

I have contracted with my personal executive coaching company, and we will be providing you with personalized attention in the form of business development tips and "tried-and-true" suggestions. I hope that you will find this information useful to your business and to you personally. We're not trying to sell you anything. I am only asking for the chance to prove myself to you as a competent professional who cares as deeply for details as you do. Interested?

Any feedback you can provide to me about these communications will be greatly appreciated; I certainly want to be respectful of your time. I look forward to the potential of working with you.

In this e-mail, we are introducing the concept of developing a mutual referral partnership. That will be explained in more detail in a later chapter, but that is the essence of why this appeals to so many people. Not only is everyone getting business tips that can make their own life easier, but the client that you represent is bringing his company's name to others on a consistent basis. Consistency makes all the difference.

Finally, you and your ready-to-roll systems are putting you in a position to be a solution provider. Your client is one busy individual. There is no way he or she can personally go around and "reach out" to all these professionals. However, these e-mails, postcards, and phone calls on a regular basis act like a new worker in the office. The beauty of it is the systems go to work without fail – no glitches. You have essentially solved their marketing problems because you are keeping in touch with the professionals they would love to have more contact with. Later we will discuss how that blossoms into professional relationships that make everyone's work load more manageable.

Conclusion

Today's companies are keenly aware of how important communication is to their survival. Ironically, keeping that communication current is very difficult. These systems make that happen without the stress. You are positioning yourself as a solution provider for both the client and his future contacts. This creates a ripple-effect result that benefits everyone. You are literally breaking ground for the client in his or her industry. More prospects will be on the way!

CHAPTER 4 - SOLVING PROBLEMS / PRESENTING SOLUTIONS

"Every problem has a gift for you in its hands." - Richard Bach

A.   Choosing your "A" list of clients
B.   How to get 30 leads and 3rd –party endorsements
C.   The sales closing ratio
D.   Meeting the needs as expressed in key questions

At this point, it is important to get into the actual methods used to accomplish the goals outlined in the first three chapters. Your referral source and/or business client is now positioned to put all the systems in action. Now it is imperative that you target your referral database in the most effective way. The core of this system is based on the fact that reaching out to the contacts will increase his or her business, salary, and exposure to the professional world. It is designed to lessen stress and client involvement and that frees your client to go on with his business while these systems work for him.

It is time to develop a list of clients. Divide all your referral sources into A, B, and C categories. "As" refer at least one client a month, "Bs" refer at least one client several times a year, and "Cs" refer at least one client a year. The average professional should have 10 As, 20 Bs, and 40 Cs. These parameters allow the systems to work efficiently. Your client is now narrowing down the field and helping you to reach out to the people who are most likely to make a difference in his or her business. Those people are being targeted for obvious reasons. Your referral source needs to understand that when he chooses that group, he is sending information to the people who can enhance his business the most. They are the most likely to reciprocate. However, you don't want to limit their ability to increase business, so you have provided a system that doesn't neglect other contacts.

Each business professional will have to evaluate his or her contacts. The referral list is very important, but it can be modified at any time. The systems will monitor the response level from these people and this will enable the client to feel as though the ones being sent the consistent information are really the ones who are responding positively. The plan is flexible.

Other national business people have found this maxim to be true. One such person is Dirk Zeller, a very knowledgeable motivational speaker and writer for the real estate industry. His ability to close sales is remarkable. He values the precept that finding an initial list of core contacts is essential. They readily recognize your (the client's) name, and they are often familiar with the client's business practices. They would be willing to share in the name recognition system as well as in the further ability to expand their own referral base. It works for everyone.

A rule every entrepreneur should know!

Which clients are essential to your business? You've probably heard of the 80/20 rule and maybe even the cluster rule. I've recently come across a new rule that I would like to share with you; it's called the 20/50/30 rule.

According to Dirk Zeller, author and sales coach,

> In the 20/50/30 rule, the top 20 percent [of your clients] are made up of the people who will do business with you easily. This 20 percent represent people with whom you have already built trust and rapport. [They are] like gold. The next group is the 50 percent who are on the fence. It takes sufficient data and reasoning to get them to commit. You just need to apply solid sales skills and these prospects will become like the original 20 percent. The final group, which is the group 30 percent of people fall into, is the most challenging and dangerous group. This group demands tremendous amounts of energy and time to convince them to join your side of the fence. A large amount of time can be invested on people in this 30 percent, but it will equate to low payoff and high frustration.

Zeller goes on to say that sales professionals who want to focus their time on the highest dollar-productive group of people should devote most of their time to the 20%, keeping them happy, asking for referrals, etc. Then work to get the 50% into that key 20%, and do everything you can to avoid the 30%. Ask yourself where each of your prospects falls and how you can move each of them to the 20%.

Generating third-party endorsements

Generating prospects from your referral sources can be a significant challenge… if you approach it in a haphazard manner. If, on the other hand, you approach prospecting in a scientific, step-by-step fashion, you will realize far greater results. Below you will find a prospecting system that will serve as a guide to you in this vital aspect of your business.

Generate 30 Great Prospects
Immediately from every referral source

Purpose

Generate $5,000 or more in sales commissions on your very first in-person meeting or your third phone call. Help all professional referral sources to see the benefit of sharing with you every prospect they have not converted in the last six months so you can help to cross-sell them.

Steps

1. Obtain answers to at least the top 3 questions (Current work hours/hours goal, sales closing ratio, WOW income goal) and work to gather all 7 key questions.
2. Let them know you can help them achieve their full potential.
3. Show them how much money they are losing & give a taste of how you can help them achieve their WOW income goals.
4. Identify two major reasons people do business with them, and then build a cross-selling script.
5. Ask them how many leads they would like you to target to cross-sell them.
6. Ask them when they believe they can have their leads from the last six months compiled.
7. Schedule the next time to get together with them, or invite them to a business development seminar.

I will work on scheduling calls to each of them over the next 30 to 60 days. Could you please identify the top 5 to 15 leads with whom I could help you the most right now? If we did this on a regular basis, it could help you increase your sales closing ratio from ____% to ____%; that would double or triple your business. What do you think about that?

OK. Let me understand what we're setting out to do together. The next time we get together, you are going to have all of your prospects from the last six months, and I'm going to work on cross-selling you with the goal of generating $25,000 or more in added income for you. Sound about right?

When would you like to schedule a time to get together so I can start working to put that $25,000 in your pocket rather than in a competitor's pocket?

This next rule you will offer a solution to your client. It expands on the principle of reaching out to more sources with a workable system.

A principle that I've really found to be true in my business is called the "cluster rule." Every client you have knows 4-6 other people who need your services, too. That means that every client and even every prospect is a potential gold mine of business and qualified leads--if you know how to mine it properly!

This cluster rule really allows for maximum expansion for everyone. People who trust you and do regular business with you are going to be the best sources you can acquire. Their endorsement sends you out to reach others. It can really be a gold mine of business.

Since you have targeted the client's most pressing needs, here is a solution that helps many in business. It gets back to the challenge of not having excess funds and excess time. This is a universal problem, and you can provide the answer:

"You said your challenge is having the funds for marketing AND having the time to do it--at the same time. Well, I've really learned that making the investment into a turnkey marketing system that just goes whether you have the time or not is what makes the funds available! See, here's the cycle of events:

*You can set up the system.

*You start maximizing your database, getting referrals from your past clients, etc.

*One or two referrals pay for the whole system.

*You get a steady stream of referrals because you've shown how much you care for past clients, no matter what the market's doing.

One thing I'd suggest is sending something relational to your past and current clients as well, even the ones who haven't moved or referred you a lead in years--don't underestimate them! Staying in touch with them even when they're no longer 'clients' will strike a real chord with them that you care more about them than just their immediate business."

The sales-closing ratio

For most business professionals, you will also be addressing the sales-closing ratio that they typically see in their business. It is such a common issue when dealing with clients. They want so much to increase that ratio because they have spent so much time leading up to the final sale. You need to provide ways to increase that ratio and thereby increase their income.

This next e-mail that is sent to people seeking help with their sales-closing ratios provides a simple way to keep those contacts visible. This is a concrete way to help your referral source remember to contact the key sales people. In other words, your systems send out a reminder that prompts an action, and the ripple effect goes on. People need some prodding. We all want results, but we are not all willing to stay at task. This solves that problem.

Here's a tip my business coach gave to me that has worked wonders with my sales calls: Plug your key sales contacts into your calendar twice a week for 3 months. Then you don't have to think about it. The reminders to call them will be automatic! It only takes a couple of minutes to get them into your calendar, and then the reminders keep popping up to place that call or drop them a note.

If you're like me, making those calls can be challenging, but realize that it is important to show confidence, so don't be afraid to be a little bolder than you're comfortable with (unless you have a tendency to overdo in that department). Remember to ask for referrals. You never know what will come of it! By the way, please do let me know if you're currently working with any clients who could use my expertise to make their transaction a little smoother.

Here's another e-mail suggestion for solving the sales-closing issue:

I found some great info that I wanted to share with you. Hope it's helpful.

If you had 10 leads, how many would you be able to write up? Sales closing ratios represent the number of leads out of that 10 that you actually are able to turn into deals. Most industries average around 10% (closing 1 out of 10 leads), so how do you size up against it? If you are at or around 10%, that means that you aren't getting paid for 90% of the work you do. OUCH! It's very hard to get to your WOW income goals at this level of sales closings. In order to improve this ratio, it always helps to improve your efforts to follow up with your prospects. A turnkey system for this follow-up can mean the difference between earning returns on your work and continuing to lose money each day.

Two key marketing strategies can help with this: a monthly newsletter system to help build relationships for you so you can spend your time on phone calls and in-person visits (which I can get you some info on if you're interested) and an automated referral development system for your key referral sources (which I can also help with).

Let me know if any of those systems or ideas meet your interest level. Based on what I mentioned, where is your sales closing ratio currently?

Often just making the referral source and/or business client aware of the statistics on sales closing ratios is a step in the right direction. These systems will provide guidelines for your referral so that he or she realizes what is normal in the industry. The tools are designed to evaluate sales patterns and set the referral source up for better returns. How many professionals have the time to analyze their business this thoroughly? Not many. That is why having these turnkey systems in place makes such a huge difference.

It is important to mention that the monthly newsletter is still a very viable method of marketing. In today's world, we gravitate toward e-mails and phone calls. Yet, a letter is often what the prospect is looking for. It provides something to hang on to and refer to in the future. Your message is being conveyed in a concrete way. My experience has shown me that the powerful triangle: in-person, phone calls, and mass outreach will keep your referral source and business client in the mainstream in his or her industry. You are providing a service that works on a consistent basis!

You have positioned yourself to address your referral source's key questions with the answers to solve his problems. Getting the referral source on board is essential. Finding ways to increase that sales-closing ratio is also pivotal. Addressing the referral source's desire to increase salary and decrease workload is all part of the equation. It is so refreshing to find a system that overlaps so efficiently. People are contacted for the referral source's behalf and the benefits begin for everyone.

Meeting the needs as expressed in key questions

Do you know people who let life drive them? By that I mean, people who organize their business and their life around all the interruptions that come their way. You might admire their spontaneity, but do you admire the results they typically get? It would be nice to think that all the desirable clients walk through the door or call on the phone, but that is terribly unrealistic. Think about a football game without a plan of attack? Scary! To fail to plan is to plan to fail. You need to get an internal perspective of your client's business to best serve their needs.

It is very wise to offer your referral source and business client some type of business assessment to determine how to best solve their business needs. It is wise to plan on spending some time with a 30-minute interview to assess your referral source's situation. Below you will find a script to help "sell" your client on the assessment and show him or her the value of this tool. One valuable free on-line tool is the Mini X-Ray. Www.synergysolutions.net

Introducing your contacts to the mini Business X-Ray

"My name is Ken Marley, and I wanted to give you a call. I've been receiving coaching to help me increase my income and decrease the number of hours I work. This has proved to be so successful for me that I have contracted with my coaching company to offer some of the same tools I use to help you increase your income and decrease the number of hours you're working.

I would like to offer you the FREE on-line mini Business X-Ray. **The mini Business X-Ray will quickly help you to identify the overall health of your business and provide suggestions that can increase your income and decrease the number of hours you work by implementing powerful systems that help your business grow even when you're not working on your business.** *It only takes around 5 minutes to do the mini X-Ray right on-line. There is no cost to you. Is that something you would be interested in? When would be the most convenient time for you?"*

Results you should expect from your systems and tools

As a side note, you may not be totally familiar with using the system until you've done at least five mini X-Rays. On average, you should receive at least four leads from every individual for whom you sponsor a mini Business X-Ray over a three- to six-month period of time. Naturally, some individuals will achieve better results than others.

Mini X-Ray: Version 3.00
Interviewer or speaker:
Location & date or date of X-Ray:

1. WOW Income: $_____ 2. Minimum $_____
3. Current number of hours worked per week: ____/wk   Goal: ____/wk
4. Sales Closing Ratio: ____%
5. Final Closing Ratio: ____%
6. Biggest Challenges: (Getting to WOW income and working minimal hours)
   a.

   b.

   6b:Which shape do you like the most:(1-most to 4) ___a. square ___b. Triangle
       ___c. squiggly line   ___d. Circle
   6c: Your birth order: _____

7. Please rate the following from 1 to 10 with 10 being the best.
   In the first ___ please rate where you are currently. In the [___] please rate where you would
   like to be.
   __ [__] a. Ability to generate business from other professionals or corporate referral sources
   __ [__] b. Results of repeat business, referrals from current clients, and profitability of current
             clients
   __ [__] c. Ability to generate a large number of qualified leads and convert them to clients
   __ [__] d. The effectiveness, profitability, and consistency of in-person sales contacts
   __ [__] e. Degree to which your business has grown as a result of phone contact with clients and
             prospects
   __ [__] f. Consistency of your relationship marketing to retain clients and generate new prospects
   __ [__] Total a through f. [54+: Great] [48-53: Good] [42-47: Below Potential]
            [Less than 42: Far Below Potential]

   __ [__]-g. Stress   __ [__]-j. Life Balance   __ [__]-m. Time management
   __ [__]-h. Follow-through __ [__]-k. Personal time   __ [__]-n. Marriage
   __ [__]-i. Spiritual life __ [__]-l. Consistency   __ [__]-o. Networking

p. Past Income: 20__:_____, 20__:_____, 20__:_____, 20__:_____
q. Number of past client you have contact data on:_____ Database using:_____
r. Would you like input, suggestions, or ideas on any of the above? [ ]-Yes, [ ]-No
Please rate in order from 1 to 4 (with 1 being the most frustrating) which of the following would cause you the most
frustration:
____ A. Things not being accurate or done correctly.
____ B. Things being out of control.
____ C. Things not being fun or exciting.
____ D. Conflict with others.

Conclusion

Everyone wants to be a problem solver. We all want to rush into the burning building and save the victims. Let's hope your client isn't really sitting in a burning building. It is comforting to know that you have started the process for the professional that will keep the embers very low. I like to think of this as the beginning of a beautiful relationship with all the parties concerned. There will be some modifications that will need to be made over the course of time, but essentially, you and your client will see many positive results. We are well on our way in this professional journey.

Part III   BRIDGE

Chapter 5 - COACHING

"How can I be useful, of what service can I be?" - Vincent Van Gogh

A.   Coaching your referral sources to become their business development resource

B.   Receiving coaching yourself

C.   Coaching your team

Receiving coaching yourself

Executive coaching is really a popular buzzword these days. It seems that everyone has a coach – movie stars, athletes, and of course, business professionals. My experience has shown me that the right coach and coaching strategies can make all the difference in the world. The accountability factor works wonders for most people because they are consistently on target with their goals and desires. The benefits are great; the drawbacks are not finding the right coach for the right job. One needs to be open to suggestions from qualified sources; however, the coaching company has to offer measurable results. Two reasons why you deserve a system that can visibly show you the results are *time* and *cost*.

To provide the best coaching for your client, you need to operate on this principle: give them the right action, in the right way, over the right period of time. This may sound a little too simplistic, but essentially you want to offer a standardized format that is based on natural laws and principles. That is the foundation that keeps everyone on the same page. You are actually offering them a whole-life plan that is both flexible and customized to fit their business. How do you accomplish this? It is by giving the client a tool that is mathematically driven to assess their progress on a monthly basis.

I have spoken with countless business people and coaches who are receptive to ways to enhance their business. The problems arise when the methods are enacted over a period of time, but no one seems to know if they are functioning properly. It is as though you stay on a low-carb diet for months, but never get on the scale to find out if it is working. The coaching that I am proposing enables both the client and the coach to numerically determine monthly if the tools are doing what they were set out to do.

Not only is it possible to determine results in a concrete way, it is wise to establish accountability coaches who can make these tools even more effective. Since you have undoubtedly realized, I function best with the teamwork approach. I find that it carries over into all facets of life and business. Individuals who subscribe to this precept get the most for their effort. For instance, everyone who wants to get the most out of a coaching experience really needs to "employ" four coaches. What is really wonderful about your "employees" is the fact that you honestly *only pay for one*. Good economics, right?

Here's a way to get the most out of coaching on a daily basis: Most of the people I deal with don't realize what sources of information and constructive criticism they have around them. Again, lose the isolationist ideology - put yourself on the team bandwagon! People do best with four coaches. The accountability is phenomenal. I have found that a person's spouse is invaluable in this process. If it is true that opposites attract, what better way to glean information from someone who can give you the other side of the coin at no cost to you. Most spouses volunteer this information, but you need to look at it as a benefit, not a worn out criticism. Bring your spouse into your business by including them in your decisions and planning. Who is next on you list of reasonably-priced coaches? Do you have children, preferably teen-agers? If you have spent any time with teens, you know that they are not suffering from a lack of honesty in their interpersonal dealings. Take advantage of sharing your business and personal goals with these truth-tellers. Get them on the team. They provide real insight and often give you a whole new perspective. Your third source can be a co-worker. Who better to understand the workings of the company. These people are in the trenches with you and can offer solutions because they truly have a vested interest in making the environment better. Last, but not least, is a professional coach. These are individuals who give you those tools that are flexible for your industry and provide measurable results on a monthly basis. Don't settle for less. You need to visually see whether or not the program is doing what it says it can do.

Coaches are all around you!

1.   Your Spouse

2.   A child in your home

3.   A co-worker

4.   A professional coach who provides MEASURABLE RESULTS

Coaching your referral sources

Putting like people and industries together to develop business and personal relationships is a worthwhile endeavor. Your desire is to take your client's referral sources and make it a viable business development source for the people it reaches out to. The ripple effect should be a perk for everyone. Therefore, you need to give them systems that are universally applicable to their industry. The business tips and suggestions need to apply to a fairly broad base. Here are some suggestions for ways to train your client to assist others in their business:

> "I'd like to share a thought-provoking principle with you today about your prospects. Most of the contacts I speak to tell me they're not following up with their leads in the most effective manner. I thought you might like to hear for free something I've been learning in my coaching sessions.
> The domino principle seems simple but can systematize your prospecting to a level most people never experience. Simply stated, it says that one thing leads to another. Successful lead tracking systems lead to proper identification of A, B, and C prospects. Categorizing prospects leads to knowing how to contact them and how often. Understanding how and when to contact them leads to the right amount of pressure and the best timing for your sales presentation, which leads (of course) to sales!
> I can offer you a lead tracking system at no charge, which will be an excellent start for you. I look forward to helping you begin a domino effect that will help you increase your income and decrease your hours at work!"

The lead tracking systems that has been developed comes from a well-honed program that kicks in for your client. It creates a domino effect that reaches out to the leads in a systematic manner that saves your client time and money. Timing is essential in this game because everyone's hours are precious. Why lose a contact and/or sale because you have either targeted the wrong contacts or chosen the wrong time to get in touch with them? Why not let an experienced coaching company give you that edge? Remember, you have built up a trusting environment. Let it go to work. Your client has to have the tools to reach out once the contacts have been established.

Now you can explain the precise techniques to open these doors. Also, the beauty of these systems rests in the fact that you or the actual client can benefit from this next method of reaching out. These systems work because they have been tested in the marketplace. You can provide the clientele to implement this tool. Here's an example of an e-mail sent by a professional who provides coaching to his top referral source:

> One thing my coaching company shared with me is that having a script DOESN'T mean you have to sound like a recording, give up your creativity and freedom in conversation, or memorize a bunch of lines like a Shakespearean actor! It simply gives you guidelines and structure where too many people have only salesmanship and a smile.

> One thing that's been helpful to me has been scripting my calls before I make them, by which I mean outlining them or having general points of reference close at hand. That does a few things for me:

> -It keeps the goal of my calls (more business!) in front of my eyes the whole time, which helps to break down reluctance.

> -It keeps me from getting too far off track on calls to "chatty" people.

> -It reminds me to weave my USP (unique selling proposition) into every call, reminding people why doing business with me is a better choice than working with a competitor.

> I think working on scripting would be a big help to you as it has for me. Remember, if you're not calling your past clients 4 times a year, you're losing money monthly! Scripting can help you get up the courage to stay on top of them.

Notice how scripting gives the client a frame of reference for future contacts. This particular message really packs a lot into it. It helps the client to stay goal centered and it encourages them to come up with a unique selling proposition – great idea! Then the clincher comes when it reminds the client to keep in touch with contacts four times a year. This is great advice. Would we all be this organized and purposeful? Probably not! It provides a visual reminder to reach the contacts called with a succinct message.

Continue to reinforce to your clients and their contacts the importance of working together. Teamwork just makes sense to me, but you have to keep in mind that many people are convinced that working alone solves problems. They want to be the only one who carries the ball down the field. This is a great hero principle, but what about all the other players on the team? You need to reinforce the principle that your systems create a web of efficiency. The domino effect keeps the program running smoothly.

One business/life development principle I've learned, the "**Two Oxen Principle**," has taught me a lot about leadership. It says that two oxen will do the work of 100, not of two. Makes you think, doesn't it? Can you think of any areas at your office where you're taking the work onto yourself instead of teaching others and coaching them to share the load? If you share this load, it will be a real win-win for both you and the other people you help because they'll learn some great leadership principles while in the process of working with you. It's like that old saying that you can either teach the kids to wash the dishes or spend the rest of your life washing them because you're afraid the kids will break one!

Now that you've considered these principles, think about the opportunity of sharing this wisdom with your clients. That is what these systems are all about. Getting people on the team takes some effort, but the dividends are astounding. We all really do benefit from the efforts of others. Take advantage of the plan! As you progress with your client, it is essential to give him or her some succinct methods to grow the business. You are providing a reservoir of information to keep people on top of their game.

People need some concrete statistics to help them gain some perspective into their business operations. Over the years, I have found that this next nugget gives people a little piece of the gold as they reflect on what is really happening in their own business. Again, the daily chores or running a business can keep professionals from looking ahead and evaluating their situation. You benefit from the tools to do that, and so do they.

DO NOT STEAL FROM YOUR BUSINESS

Business coaches normally recommend that individuals invest somewhere between 10% and 20% back into the development of their business. Many individuals say they don't believe they are making enough to do that. If you think along those lines, one of three things is probably going to be true:

1. You are going to have wide business cycles, and your business will cause you stress.
2. You're going to earn a great deal less than the time you put in is worth.
3. You're going to level off in your personal income and have less than 15% income growth each year, rather than the 30% to 50% that is possible with the right systems in place.

The theory here is that "business theft" is going on right under people's noses. Aren't we always so convinced that others are taking our time and money? Well, the others aren't always to blame.

Most sales professionals are stealing and don't even realize it. The following are some of the key indicators of business theft:

1. You have a consistent income or your income growth is less than 15% for two or more years in a row.

2. You feel a great deal of stress in your life, and much of that stress arises from your business.
3. You are working more hours than you would like.
4. You envision great ideas and business opportunities but fail to follow through with them.
5. You have an instinctive feel that you're not living up to your full potential.

6. You are working more hours than you would like.
7. You envision great ideas and business opportunities but fail to follow through with them.
8. You have an instinctive feel that you're not living up to your full potential.

9. You feel a great deal of stress in your life, and much of that stress arises from your business.
10. You are working more hours than you would like.
11. You envision great ideas and business opportunities but fail to follow through with them.
12. You have an instinctive feel that you're not living up to your full potential.

All of these "theft" problems get back to not making the most of the time we are handed daily. Doesn't this bring home the need for systems that keep a client and his contacts focused?

Five things to do EVERY DAY to build your referral sources:

1. Make three phone calls per day. Ask what people's challenges are and find ways to bring solutions.

2. Implement ONE turnkey mailing system for your whole database.

3. Help professional referral partners send mailings every month without any cost to you.

4. Get 60 hours worth of work done while only working 30 hours a week. Get systems to do your work for you.

5. Communicate to referral sources 300 times a month without doing any work

Relationships build business

Relationship marketing can be huge for referral business and creating long-term sources of referrals. It's extremely effective because it builds on or works to create a relationship rather than explaining products and services or the seller.

Monthly newsletter systems that come from you and invite calls to you but aren't JUST about your business are one key way to do relationship marketing. When you set up a mailing or newsletter system, don't set out to explain your products/services in every letter; worry about that once you've built a relationship. People do business based on relationships much more than on products and services, even when they're the best in the industry. Build relationships for several months through your mailings, then move to phone and in-person contacts where you will want to explain your products and services.

All of these suggestions bring out the importance of building good solid relationships with your referral sources. It provides a total turnkey operation to make sure that no one falls through the cracks – the client or his contacts. The accountability factor is wonderful.

I think we can all agree that it is important to be fed so that we can hand out food to others. I would strongly recommend an accountability program. I have found several ways to keep my skills sharp so that I can be of service to other professionals. As a professional coach, I keep abreast of the newest literature on business principles. I would like to suggest the following authors as excellent sources for running businesses well. These individuals give thorough overviews on today's business practices. The tools I have developed are designed to meet the needs of individual business professionals; however, we all gain from keeping

High-Trust Selling	by Todd Duncan
Killing the Sale	by Todd Duncan
The Power of Positive Thinking	by Norman Vincent Peale
The Purpose Driven Life	by Rick Warren
The Myth of Leadership	by Jeffrey S. Nielsen

I have found these books to be very beneficial. Just taking the time to read them will enrich your professional life and your business. They have inspired me and given me concrete ways to reach out to my client base with helpful ideas and suggestions.

Sending the coaching message out to professionals is something I thoroughly enjoy doing. Once the trust factor has been established, these professionals are receptive to ways to improve their business. As outlined earlier, the tools are already in place and functioning for the client. I make sure that these tools are functioning properly on a monthly basis by using graphs and charts that visibly show the results. Now we can focus on the direct ways to make his or her business operate more effectively. The communication process goes right on functioning for your client – leads are being created, people are being contacted on a regular basis, and e-mails and mailings continue. Behind the scenes operations are in full progress. It is vitally important, however, to keep the client on top of his or her game.

Coaching your team

Your client is now in a unique position to pass on the torch with these systems. Not only will the means of communication continue to their referral sources, but the client can impart real quality-of-life precepts to help their co-workers and their referral sources. These tools are designed to be so solidly based on natural laws and precepts that they can assist others in getting the most out of their time and effort. Since you and your client are so intent on minimizing time and effort, doesn't it make sense to pass on these principles to others so that they can benefit? I have seen deep and binding relationships that were created because this approach puts people on the same page. It gives everyone a better quality of life. How can you and your client offer the benefits of these tools to others without incurring additional cost? Think about partnering with a non-profit organization. I'll explain.

As a result of all the tools that have been developed, it seemed very wise and philanthropic to partner with a non-profit organization. This may take some work initially and won't payoff right away but over time they can bring like-minded individuals together and you can accomplish a great deal together. Fortunately, all the natural laws and principles apply in both the business and the non-business/community/non-profit world. Isn't it grand to think about a tool that can join people with mutual interests? Again, the teamwork concept drives the process. We do benefit from others!

As a coached individual, you can use this non-profit organization, at no cost, to connect people who are interested in building their referral base. You can think of it as another spoke to the wheel that makes a business run smoothly. It can run at no additional cost, and that is a perk for everyone. To be able to give your team and your referral sources this kind of value is terrific. Your team is handing out information to others that can directly benefit their business while keeping your business goals in mind for others.

Conclusion

If the expression "one hand washes the other" is true, and I think it is, then coaching should touch everyone's life in a worthwhile way. Setting up an accountability group with people that you deal with directly is wise as it enables you to hear about all sides of the equation. Having a coaching company that offers a measurable device to determine if you are reaching your targets is the best case scenario. With those forces in place, you can be a "provider" for your team and your referral base with the ideas you have learned and implemented. Also, being able to tap into a non-profit organization enables you to reach out with the message without incurring any more cost. The entire team scores a touchdown!

Part IV   MANAGING YOUR TEAM

Chapter 6 - HIRING AND COMPANY GOALS

"The laborer is worthy of his hire." - Luke 10:7 (New Testament)

A.   Personalities – choosing the right people based on the four personality types

B.   The assembly line of sales

C.   Casting the vision of the company

At this point it is important to discuss the hiring process. Through the years I have gathered a great deal of information about various personality types. I find that my knowledge of these personality types has greatly influenced my hiring techniques and methods. Since this information is extensive, I have endeavored to break it into workable segments so that professionals can access the information and use it to their best advantage. Not unlike the other systems I have previously addressed, being knowledgeable in personality types helps all parties. Everyone comes out ahead when we learn to position people based on their inherent skills and attitudes. I am sure this will be instructional and helpful. The intent here is to give you a handle on these four types and then give you some tools to measure those traits in the people you work with on a daily basis.

Observing people is really an intriguing enterprise. Over the years I have found that people filter into four main groups. Please be assured, many people overlap these characteristics. We are all very unique individuals. However, it is wise to look for the following major personality groups when you or your client seeks individuals to make his or her company operate efficiently:

ANALYTICAL –

This type of individual is most content when he or she can avoid mistakes. They look at work-related activities as challenges that should be mapped out and tackled in an orderly fashion. They thrive on order, schedules, and outlines. Remember the early days of school? Think back to the individual who came to class with all his supplies on the first day. Did that person seem a little too organized? Well, that is the best mode for this individual. Analytical people desire a great deal of data. They want to ensure that they have enough data to prove that they made the right decision. They hate to be wrong and therefore tend to take a lot of time in making decisions. Obviously, these types can focus so intensely on the details that the big picture gets lost. Yet, think of the advantages of hiring such an individual to handle the details of your firm? These people make sure that all the knots are tied. I tend to think of them as the types who enjoy bookkeeping, scheduling, consistent calling, and the like. They can be indispensable to a company or a client who desperately needs order. Don't expect them to quickly implement a new idea that has just popped up. This is not their strong suit. They don't get caught up in the "do it now" method. They thrive on a methodical process.

DRIVER –

Want to get it done? Need the ball carried down the field NOW? Hire a driver. These people come in with an innate desire to get the place moving and take control. They will instinctively tell you that they are ready for the challenge – whatever it is! These people can really think on their feet. The word multitasked comes to mind immediately. Flip back into time to the child who told the coach he or she could play any position offered. The technical rules of the sport weren't really that important. This person wants to be a part of the game. Obviously, other associates may see this individual as the type who jumps into the fray without asking enough questions, but often this person can literally solve the problems as they happen. Enthusiasm abounds with these types, and it can be very contagious for others working with them.

EXPRESSIVE –

These personality types also tend to see the big picture and gravitate to multiple ideas. They can readily switch direction and not be overwhelmed. This type loves people-oriented tasks. Expressive people look for fun and creative ways to solve company issues. When these people are "on", they are really "on." Envision the person who lands that big sale and is literally on top of the world on Monday; however, on Tuesday the same person may be totally out of energy. How did I ever clinch that deal? I am exhausted today. It is an up and down process, but the expressive definitely brings energy and life to a firm. They do want to get the job done.

AMIABLE –

This is the person on the playground who brings all the kids together for a "fun" game of kickball. Keeping everyone happy during the game is their primary goal. They aren't big risk takers because their goal is to keep peace and harmony at a premium. Conflict is not their happy place. They will avoid this at all cost. This can be a disadvantage when they are put in a situation where it is necessary to evaluate other employees or "shake up the ranks" and put people in other situations. This can disrupt their harmony code. They do have the ability to bring the people together for group tasks that require a team approach. This is the instance where these people really shine. Others respond to their cooperative spirit and desire for cohesiveness.

As you read this, you probably saw yourself in all four types. That is the beauty of focusing on these main categories. There are definite overlaps on everyone's part. People aren't just one type exclusively. When you are looking for people to hire and work with, however, it does help to see where the individual's strengths lie. We all bring something to the table at a job and you want to get the most out of the person while allowing him or her to work in the best environment possible. It is a two-way street.

Using the following tool to determine the person's personality traits would be helpful. This is a measurable tool to assist you in helping them focus on their strengths and weaknesses:

Could I get you to take two minutes to fill out this really brief personality "test?" I wanted to be able to give you some insights into your own personality and how you can improve your most valued relationships. Thanks so much!

Please place a 1 by the response that is most like you and a 2 by the response you'd be the second most likely to choose.
Which of the following would cause you the most frustration?
__ A. When something is not done correctly, in order, or the way it should be done.
__ B. When something is out of control.
__ C. When things aren't fun and exciting.
__ D. When people are upset or angry.

Draw the following objects on scrap paper. Which do you like the most?
A. square   B. triangle   C. curvy squiggle   D. circle

Which of the following statements is most like you?
__ A. I like to have things in order and done right the first time.
__ B. I like it when people have goals and are moving forward-- fast!
__ C. I like it when everyone is having a great time and I'm having FUN!
__ D. I like it when the team is working well together.

       Thanks for taking the initiative to find out more about improving yourself and your relationships!

There are more complicated tests to determine people's personality traits, but by keeping it simple, you aren't being intimidating to your client or his employees. It gives you the opportunity to find out basic likes and dislikes to help you with the hiring process. Also, it can greatly assist you after the individual is hired because you will be better equipped to work efficiently and cooperatively with this individual.

As a professional, you want to look at the whole person when you hire. I have found that looking for some basic attitudes in a perspective employee really puts everyone on the same page. These techniques can focus the individual and give the employer a good overview of the person and their aspirations. Here are some of the key questions to ask:

1.   What does success in life mean to you?

2.   How would you like to be managed within this job?

3.   What is your greatest strength?

4.   What is your greatest weakness?

5.   What are your income goals?

6.   Do you possess a strong work ethic?

7.   Do you have strong values?

8.   Do you consider yourself a loyal employee?

9.   Are you a disciplined person?

10.   Are you willing to take action on your decisions?

It has been my observation that these are key issues that need to be addressed in the hiring process. By using a personality test and asking the above questions, a business professional will have a very good understanding of the desired employee. To make this process even more efficient, I have developed media CDs and DVDs that explain the purpose of the company and its goals. Also, an information/training phone line has been set up to give the new people a chance to get their questions answered.

Once the individual comes onboard, it is wise to make sure that you have a training manual in place to give them the assistance they need. My company operates well with the benefits of a computer program that allows the employees to access this information online. As previously stated, the goal is to allow the systems to operate without the client (professional) having to be overly involved in the process. It keeps the focus centralized for everyone.

Assembly Line of Sales

Now that you have zeroed in on the personality types within a company, it is time to explain an efficient method to move sales to a new level. Basically, this method functions very much like a history timeline. Each facet has a part to play in the final sale. There are three main points to consider: pre-sales, sales, and post-sales. In the pre-sale phase you are emphasizing the phone calls, e-mails, and having the clients answer the seven key questions that your employees have been trained to asked. Accomplishing the sale is the goal and that occurs midway through this process. After the sale, as you have promised, the servicing begins in earnest. You will be giving your clients the follow-up calls and e-mails, the evaluations, and the continued marketing to keep them informed about new and useful products. If you are focusing on making your business make a profit without you, it is essential that your employees understand this process very well. It should literally flow. You, the professional, have explained the process to the employees, and they have been empowered to carry out the process. People are on the same page.

The leader of the company has to be aware that learning and mastering these techniques are two different things. It is understood that it takes some time to become proficient in following the assembly line to completion. However, once it is mastered, the results come in for both the client and the company leader. It benefits everyone. Having these systems ready to roll is the key to making the profit without continual involvement.

Casting the vision of the company

It is fair to say that the president or head business professional of a firm sets the tone for the entire company. I am sure we can all think of very famous people such as Lee Iococa, formerly of Chrysler Corporation, Michael Eisner, who worked for Disney Corporation, and Donald Trump, real estate magnate, who are total tone setters. Their attitude about business is what makes the wheels turn at their firms. These three men have made some inspirational remarks that can be pondered a bit in the world of business. Lee Iacocca said: "He who thinks he's leading but has no one following him is just taking a walk. Michael Eisner is quoted as saying: "If it's not growing, it's going to die." Donald Trump remarked, "As long as you are going to be thinking anyway, think big."

Take a moment to reflect on having any of these three businessmen for a boss. Can you get a glimpse of their vision by just contemplating those quotes? Actually, they speak volumes about the ideologies of these individuals.

Think about what represents your ideology. Take some time to assess what matters to you personally and what your hopes for the future are. This will help you to formulate some concrete thoughts on what the company means to you and to your employees.

I would encourage you to get a mission statement for your firm. This is a statement that encompasses your dreams and desires for your company. It would also be wise to ask others, like that coaching foursome you have, what they think your company's vision is. I am sure that your spouse, children, and employees have some opinions on this. Choosing a mission statement is not only confined to the business world. Think about this statement: Where children come first. This is a statement from a local school district. Does it impact how they view their best product – the kids? I would think so. That statement is saying that all their policy decisions, hiring choices, and future plans are designed around the premise that the children are paramount in the district. This is a worthy goal. It does influence their decisions. Your mission statement needs to be worthy, too. How do you accomplish this?

Have you taken the time to reflect on where you want to be in five, ten, or fifteen years? Is your company just staying afloat or is there a vision to sail into the future with pride? Have you consulted that coaching base and asked them where they think the ship is headed and for whom is the business designed? These are lofty and philosophical discussions, but I guarantee you they will bring you back to what is really important to you and your firm. It is fundamentally the reason why you go to work each day and why you have asked others to join you on this journey. You will value the time you spend formulating that mission statement. Some business professionals I know have taken the time to place that statement in their office, made it a part of their stationery, or placed it on their business cards. All of these are great ideas. Keep the mission clear and attainable. Your employees will be inspired to do better as a result of it.

- A mission statement should say who your company is, what you do, what you stand for and why you do it.
- An effective mission statement is best developed with input by all the members of an organization.
- The best mission statements tend to be 3-4 sentences long.
- Avoid saying how great you are, what great quality and what great service you provide.

- Examine other company's mission statements, but make certain your statement is you and not some other company. That is why you should not copy a statement.

- Make sure you actually believe in your mission statement, if you don't,

Conclusion

Bringing the right people to the right job is really a satisfying prospect. It seems to bring out the best in everyone. Taking some time to evaluate the personalities of perspective employees is a wise method of directing the people to the right occupation. It really serves everyone's purpose. Using a simple test can make all the difference in the world to an employer who is trying to best place an individual. Also, the assembly line of sales is an efficient timeline that keeps everyone at task. All the parties involved are informed about the next step of the process. While implementing all of the above techniques, keep in mind the overall vision of the company. Make sure that all the people who seek employment with you are clear on your vision. It sets the tone for future success.

Chapter 7 - Training and pre-sales leads

"There is nothing training cannot do. Nothing is above its reach. It can turn bad morals to good; destroy bad principles and recreate good ones; it can lift men to angelship." - Mark Twain

A.   Delegating – how to do that and improve follow-through
B.   Passing on your knowledge
C.   Giving your team the tools they need

Delegating - how to do that and improve follow through

Are you ready to lead the troops into battle? Not everyone is equipped with the necessary skills to mobilize the team. This is typically the side of the desk we haven't been on. By that I mean, we are all used to following directions from teachers, coaches, and bosses, but actually give out orders ourselves? Well, that is another story entirely. This situation very much reminds me of the arm-chair quarterbacks who love to sit back and comment on all the mistakes the head coach has made. Why make that play at that time? Why use that particular player? Haven't we all been there? With the systems that have been set up; however, now is the time to get out of the chair and start your team down the field. Why bother delegating at all? There are many reasons, but two really stand out. You need to continue with the efficiency of the systems that have been set up; you are a part of the well-oiled wheel that will make your business operate. Also, you are providing excellent opportunities for your team members to learn and to be a part of the success of your company. It is a shared responsibility.

Unfortunately, I have seen many business professionals who are very reluctant to allow their team to carry the responsibility with them. Essentially, they are afraid of letting it go. They are thoroughly convinced that they need to be directly involved in all the workings of the company. Somehow not supervising every move seems irresponsible, and they insist on being a part of everything that goes on. This can really slow down productivity and cause the professional to burn out quickly. It simply uses too much of his or her valuable energy and time. There is a better way.

As mentioned in the last chapter, a team that is adequately trained will bring a lot of value to the business professional. Let's operate on the assumption that your team, whether you are functioning as a coach or an independent business professional, is well trained and understands the main purpose of the company. Let's also assume that you have naturally had a private meeting with the individual when they were hired and that the company's mission statement and future plans were discussed. Let's be honest; most of us in a new situation feel that the initial meetings have really only scratched the surface.

The team member is glad to be a part of something, and it sounds logical, but there is always so much more to learn. This is when the delegating really takes hold. Much of what I am about to explain will depend on the size of the company involved, but the principles are the same. As a leader in a professional capacity, your best play on the field is connecting the right people together to get the most out of your team. Let me set up a typical scenario.

Let's picture ourselves in an office that has approximately 25 people. Since we are focusing on making a profit while not being directly involved in every move, we have to train that team to function efficiently. In previous chapters we have stressed the importance of evaluating personalities, receiving coaching from four main sources, and reaching out to viable referral sources to make a business grow. We need to realize that the new person sees an operation that is humming along. How does that all happen? This size office would be best served by having product managers who direct the individual phases of operation.

Again, this makes a team approach work. Your new person should be slotted into his or her area of expertise and know exactly who to report to for daily direction. The professional should be confident that those leaders, usually four to five, will keep their department functioning well.

Match the task with the right person, and the wheels keep turning. Obviously, our professional will need to be informed about the workings of the department, but this will come from the department head. Do you see some meetings coming along? Yes, that is true, but the goal is to bring the major issues to the company head, not all the minor problems.

I do want to take a moment to explain the importance of praise is operating a company. Too often the meetings focus around all the troubles a department is facing. There should definitely be a time for discussing the accomplishments.

As an example: Take a moment to ponder the "Job Well Done" bonus. I firmly believe that every professional should build that perk into their office setting, and it really should be attainable! It may seem a little ridiculous to give out awards for merely completing a task, but people respond to the acknowledgement that the effort was rewarded. I would recommend keeping this simple. Give out a certificate for a lunch at a local restaurant, treat the most successful team to some donuts, or give out some movie certificates. How often do you do this?

That is something your team should discuss, but I would recommend the department leader making the decision about the winner. You are delegating an enjoyable task. You have put yourself in the midst of many famous business people who regularly celebrate the accomplishments of their staff. Don't underestimate this addition to your delegating. People perform better when they know the team appreciates their work.

Wouldn't it be lovely if all the teams that you are delegating tasks to functioned efficiently because they have been well trained, and you are regularly rewarding them within their department for good work? This would be that perfect world none of us live in, but would like to visit for a while.

There will be glitches, hurt feelings, foul-ups, and everything in between. How do you delegate in those difficult situations? Personally, I feel strongly that whatever can be handled within a working department is best handled there. It builds teamwork and understanding at that level, and you the business professional can allow the company to operate without your constant intervention. My experience has told me that getting the team to that point isn't always a smooth process. However, if you have placed the right people in the right jobs, knowing their personalities and desires, the team can become a strong force quite quickly.

I once had someone relate this team approach to me from another workplace besides the business world. See if you can draw the similarities. The "team" was created by the person in charge of the building. Each team had approximately nine members. These members were not put there by choice, but by their expertise, at the discretion of the person in charge. This particular group had never worked in a setting like this before. They were used to their independence, but now found themselves forced to meet daily, coordinate all activities as a team, and send a team leader to the person in charge for a monthly meeting. These individuals were very much used to making their own decisions about planning, scheduling, and organizing. That came to a grinding halt when they literally had to function as a team. The person in charge, who had been in their previous position at one time, found it easy to delegate--but not so easy to watch it happen. Quite frankly, he was afraid to sit in on the early meetings because everyone was so new at the process. There was a real jostling for authority as the members wanted their views to be heard and acted upon. The tension was evident. Not everyone was happy with the arrangement. As time went on, the team learned quickly to pull together or literally watch the ship go down. The main leader wisely let the team solve the initial issues before he came on the scene. He also had the advantage of watching several teams go through this developmental phase. It brought new meaning to the phrase, "we all learn at our own rate."

Picture this "team" several months into the process. Did they fail? Did the leader hide in his office to avoid the arguments? Did some people jump ship? Luckily none of that happened. They knew they had to make the system work.

You, as a business professional can see that the process of putting people together for a common goal has the same consequences in almost any setting. You the leader have to set clear goals, build in rewards, and meet with the department heads to make sure the teams are doing well. See yourself as a facilitator, not a manipulator - your teams will thank you.

Passing on your knowledge

In my estimation, this is the area where a true business professional really makes a difference in the workings of a company. Most people will follow a person who gives them direction because they realize that is the reason they get a paycheck; however, ideally passing on the knowledge you possess makes for an operation that shares your vision and desire. That is a worthy goal!

I shared the following quote with my employees to show them how I function effectively. I want to pass on this knowledge to my employees and business associates. We are all working for the good of all.

"Over the years I have found that by practicing these twelve principles, it helps in every area of my life. I trust you will consider applying these principles to your life as well. I believe if you do that, you to will find them to assist you as much as they have assisted me."

-- Mark A. Boersma

TWELVE PRINCIPLES FOR BUSINESS

1. Walls of Opportunities

2. No Problems, Only Opportunities

3. Ideal or Nothing

4. Time/Priorities

5. Thinking, Not Knowing

6. Great vs. Good - Setting GREAT goals and sometimes only getting good results.

7. The Lucky 13 Rule

8. Value in life. (Choices/consequences, values, and congruencies)

9. Roller coaster mystery

10. Stewardship (The more we do for others the more we personally gain)

11. Focus: Get better results with less effort

12. Never Quit: No mistakes, just learning opportunities

The twelve fundamental principles above are really the core to my success. They have been my compass throughout my business career. Let me give you a brief explanation of these to show you how they apply to daily business operations.

Walls of Opportunities: Every person faces challenges in his or her business. I have found it absolutely essential to look at these "walls" as challenges that I can overcome. I teach my team to find ways to go around, under, behind, or over those walls. The main thrust is an attitude that says: I will find a way.

No problems, only opportunities: As a coach who is helping others make their businesses more efficient without all the personal input, I have to teach people the benefit of looking at life situations as opportunities. It is a proven fact that the leader, coach or individual at a company sets the entire tone for the office. The attitude they convey filters down to everyone. Opportunities are good things that can be handled and enjoyed. That's the message one wants to send.

Ideal or nothing: This is for all the personality types, usually the drivers, who have the best plan and expect everyone to follow that lead. Woe to everyone if the plan isn't executed exactly as the person hoped. This is an unreal expectation! You and your team need to come to grips with the fact that seeking perfection in every move is totally unproductive. It can be crippling to think that waiting for the perfect moment is the ONLY time a team or business professional can act. That moment may never come.

Time/priorities: Schedules are filled to the max these days, but one basic fact remains - we find time for what is really important to us. This has been proven countless times. People can put down 10 things to do and only finish five; however, the five they choose will be the ones they valued. In business, one has to choose items that will bring in the most results. Having systems that work while you are working is an excellent way to see more priorities function as you prioritize your time. It is essential that you prioritize!

Thinking, not knowing: This is best explained in a common situation in most businesses. Ask an individual what he or she thinks about a topic and often you will get this, "I don't really know. I need to think about it." As a professional, I realize that the answer may seem reflective and even polite, but it isn't the right answer. You need to develop a team that does know the answer and is willing to answer for the results. It produces ownership and responsibility on everyone's part.

Great vs. good: Is it easier to settle for something that is merely good? Many would say yes. However, your goal as a business professional is to reach for the great goals. Too often people quit just before accomplishing the ultimate goal. I could give countless examples, but take a moment to think about the individual who has one semester of college left and decides to leave. Don't we all wonder why? The graduation day was in sight. Don't quit as you see yourself heading to the finish line.

The Lucky 13 Rule: This is really a fun rule to live by because it operates on the premise that the good comes back to us, often in the smallest actions we take on a daily basis. If you take a positive action with a prospect or a team member that produces two more positive actions, before you know it you have produced 13 positive actions from one. This is a great ripple effect for everyone.

Value in Life: We all make choices in our lives on a daily basis. It has been my observation that what we really value predestines those choices. Knowing what is important to you really helps with this principle; it will govern your life. I highly recommend writing down those basic values because they are really determiners of our actions and desires.

Roller Coaster Mystery: This model in business operates just like as trip to an amusement park. A business person typically begins with much enthusiasm and drive; consequently, sales go up and so does confidence. Unfortunately, that same person can't sustain that level of productivity and the roller coaster comes down. Now the person is discouraged and starts pumping in more time and effort again. It can be tiring because the cycle approach can really wear a person out. Consistency would be a better method.

Stewardship: This word conjures up many thoughts. Who is really in charge? I believe that the people who take their "gifts" seriously are able to reap the most benefits. The individuals who take responsibility for what has been given to them are the ones who are the most willing to share those gifts with others. The five "T's" to stewardship are Time, Talents, Treasurer, Trust, and Truth.
Your personal talents and attributes should be valued and then they can be handed out to help your team and associates grow.

Focus: Watching systems operate for you to increase your business is the way to focus. By setting the correct systems in place, you can literally be a part of forming more business referrals and contacts without all the personal effort. This keeps your company on track.

Never quit; no mistakes, just learning opportunities: If you hear the dreaded words, "You're fired!" (just like the *Apprentice* people on TV), you can retreat and head for the hills of shame. Or you can learn some valuable lessons. All famous people who have reached the top will tell you that the road had many bumps and tire blowouts. When you view those bumps as opportunities to gain experience and have the intelligence to not repeat the same process, you are the winner. A great deal can be learned from a failure. Keep going!

These are twelve major precepts to live by in business, and they have greatly influenced me. My team is very familiar with them and knows that they govern my life and business dealings. It is how I can best pass on my knowledge to my team. It puts us on the same page because they know how I deal with the challenges that will come up. This is all an extension of the mission statement for the company and it further explains the precepts that govern the business.

Giving your team the tools they need

A wise business professional will be sure to outfit their workers with the necessary tools to make the business run well without constant watching. Since we have discussed the importance of putting the right individual in the right position, it is essential that they feel equipped to use the tools that are provided. I have worked with several ways to accomplish this. People's personalities adjust best to certain methods; however, I find that basically the tools have to be consistent and well engineered.

As an example, I give my newly hired people the opportunity to use our training audios and developed Internet links to broaden their understanding of the company's goals and working processes. I have been very conscientious about taping via video and audio most of my presentations to other business professionals. I feel that these sessions can be beneficial to the audience I am reaching as well as the people in my office. It literally gives everyone an opportunity to hear the daily workings of the firm. Also, I have placed my training tools on my company website so that any employee can access the information he or she needs. This truly promotes an open-door policy that saves time for everyone. My intent is to make the business more efficient and workable. Since my employees can access the company's information at any time, this keeps the efficiency high. How could an individual business owner use this technique?

First and foremost, the tools that we previously talked about to reach out to the business professional's referral sources – in-person, phone, and mass outreach (mailings, e-mailing, radio, etc.) - are three of the primary tools that need to be put in place so that the individual owner can be freed up to make his or her firm more profitable.

These continue on while the professional keeps on working to make his employees more responsive and build his own private business. Through the coaching sessions that are a part of the process, I would recommend an accountability program for the professional's business. Keeping people on the same page when it comes to running a business is essential. Now we have the benefit of CDs, phone conferencing, and videos, and we can literally bring the message to larger groups at one time.

Conclusion

This chapter has truly given the business professional a chance to make it all work. By delegating, he or she can see how well the employees carry about the mission. This frees up the professional for the important tasks to be done.

Having the right people carry out the goals is the ultimate purpose here. Also, the knowledge you have acquired needs to be passed on to the employees. This assures a team that works together for the same purpose. Finally, one has to be confident that the tools are readily available for the team at all times.

Well-trained individuals make the workload tolerable for everyone. No one is feeling unprepared or unsupported. Meanwhile, the company goes forward. The tools are really the backbone of the entire production.

Chapter 8 – LEADING

"The only test of leadership is that somebody follows."   - Robert K. Greenleaf
A.   Reinforcing the vision
B.   Seeking feedback
C.   Employee appreciation
D.   Balance of perspective

Reinforcing the vision

People will enter your company as employees with the best intentions of carrying out their individual jobs correctly; however, the leader does have the obligation to keep the torch burning so that everyone realizes why they are working there in the first place. There are many ways to accomplish this goal. The problem comes when the leader fails to realize that the vision is what can really motivate everyone.

Not long ago I was watching a TV program with a famous actress. Naturally everyone at the studio thought that she had the idyllic life of fame and fortune. She has performed in countless movies, most of which are very popular and funny. Her parents were both famous, and it would appear that she had all the advantages necessary for a great Hollywood career. Yet, she began to relate her years of alcohol addiction and how it had so adversely affected her family and her life. That was a shock to most of the audience. They saw a lovely actress who even found the time to write children's books.

Her story was unique to me on many levels. First, I wasn't expecting the revelation about her addiction. Second, I didn't expect to hear a "vision to live by" from her that initially seemed too simplistic, but has remained with me ever since. She told the audience about her years of counseling and rehab to bring her to the point that she is today. Next she related a quote that one of the doctors had given her, and she said it had changed her life. She definitely had the crowd's interest. She said that she faced each challenge this way: I *GET* TO DO THIS JOB; NOT I *HAVE* TO DO THIS JOB. The actress went on to say that the simple verb change in the sentence had revolutionized her thinking. No longer did she face life with a "have to" mentality. She felt privileged and honored to have been chosen. She meant to use that mantra for every job that crossed her path. Her goal is to impart it to her children, people who often don't want to do jobs. This lady wants to make life into a gift to be shared and treasured.

As I said, at first it seemed rather simple and a little too trite, but it has stayed with me. The more I think about it, the more it can positively impact the jobs I "get" to do each day. It is fundamentally a 180 degree turnabout from a view that previously made work a chore, not a joy.

Your goal as a leader is to make your company's vision lasting and simple. It shouldn't be complicated and hard to attain. People should feel success daily with the main premise. How do you get that across, you ask? How about some clever memos or e-mails to the staff reminding them of the vision. How about a company banner that is proudly displayed that shows the importance of this goal? How about a suggestion box that allows people to write ways they saw the vision happen? Then take those comments and send them on to everyone. Names aren't necessary. The emphasis should be on the team approach to reaching the goal. Focus on getting the team behind the project. A small bonus like a free coffee at Starbucks could be awarded to the cleverest goal-getter of the week. These are just simple ways to keep the vision on the table at all times. People respond to sharing ideas.

Seeking feedback

Here's an area that requires some thought on the part of the leader. I will relate to you the ways I think this can best be accomplished, but one has to take their own and other's personalities into account when this matter comes up. First of all, I think it is essential to open yourself and your company up to feedback. Obviously, any paying client has the right to express his feelings about that wonderful product you are offering. You need to listen intently to those comments. Also, be sensitive to a client's time restraints. You have asked many key questions, and you need to design a tool for feedback from a client that doesn't consume his day. Actually, the model that seems to work best is a simple one-page evaluation sheet that covers the products you are offering to that client. Give them space to tell it like it is. Honesty is the best policy here. You want to keep them as a client, and their concerns need to be expressed openly. Some clients would prefer an oral feedback session. If that is the case, be sure you take good notes or tape the conversation with their permission. Sometimes we go back and review the comments and really realize what the person was saying. This takes a little time on our part.

Keep the process fresh and easy. By that I mean, ask questions that truly apply to their *current* situation – don't keep asking the same questions. Keep it easy by making the process quick and efficient. You want them to be honest, but they can't be expected to realign their entire firm. That isn't the purpose. If you have developed a genuine relationship with this person, the feedback process will go smoothly. Be open to allowing other employees the privilege of getting the feedback too. Sometimes a client will feel freer to open up with a different member of the team. Talk this over with your team and get their input as well.

Does a leader need feedback about his performance within a company? Yes, yes, and yes. If a leader is really interested in sharing the vision with as many individuals as he can, if he wants team members devoted to the cause on a daily basis, and if he expects his clients and friends to feel the ripple effect of this commitment, then yes, he needs to be open to feedback. I guess explaining this by using numbers would be the best way to make the point. Let's assume that just you and your spouse start a company. You two are, of course, madly in love, so the goals and dreams just mesh beautifully! The company thrives. Now it is time to add more employees so that the couple can literally get on with their personal lives. The plot is about to thicken. The new employees are ready to go and anxious to carry out the plan; however, they bring a host of new personalities and ideas to the company. This is good? Right? Yes, it is good, but it will require you the leader to understand that all these personalities bring different mini "visions" to the company. As you keep adding more employees, the variety escalates, and you will find yourself needing some direction. You need to hear from the employees directly so that you can keep the vision alive and thriving. Having more people on your team means be willing to listen to their thoughts and concerns to make the company a total success.

I recommend an evaluation of the leader every six months or on a yearly basis. I am totally in favor of keeping this simple and non-judgmental. It is not meant to be a threat to either side. The employees should be able to express their feelings with anonymity and the leader shouldn't feel as though he was just sent to the Supreme Court. The kind of evaluation that is generally most effective is one that is fairly generic. By that I mean, I would literally use a one or two-page form that is used in large firms to find out how the leader is reaching his employees. You may need a few tweaks along the way, but keeping it simple accomplishes many things. It gives the employee a quick and easy way to assess his leader and the workings of the firm. And it gives the leader a simple and fairly non-intrusive overview of the "climate" in the office. One has to be open and honest about this. If one area, such as "freedom to give suggestions", keeps coming up, it is time to reflect. If most employees think more sick days or personal days might be more beneficial, it is again time to reflect. I chose these two because of their universal nature. Most people want to be heard, and most people think they deserve a break once in a while.

Here are a few items that should appear on the evaluation:

1. Do you feel as though your comments are heard in the company?

2. Do you think the overall atmosphere of the firm creates a pleasant and productive working environment?

3. Do you feel the insurance programs and benefits within the firm meet your needs?

4. Do you feel that the holiday/personal day accommodation is adequate for a full-time employee?

5. Do you feel the vision of this company is clear and that it is being achieved daily?

6. Do you feel that your salary is equal to the effort and time you devote to the company?

7. Do you feel that the team meetings are profitable and fairly run?

8. Do you feel the company is moving in the right direction?

9. Do you want to be considered for an additional or different job within the company?

These are a few of the basic questions that can be asked and shared with the leader. This will give the leader a very good feeling regarding the satisfaction factor among the team members. It isn't a personal vendetta, but it does give people a chance to assess their work environment.

Our overall purpose is to make a company run efficiently without you the leader being overly involved. These evaluations actually enhance that process. If your employees are being utilized correctly and feel they are working in a hospitable environment, the systems work so much better. Communication is the key.

Obviously, the leader is free to set up periodic evaluations of his or her employees. The research seems to suggest that this should be more often that just once a year. My personal feeling is that seeing people in their individual work setting is the best way to assess their progress. Go out into the office and watch it happen! People shouldn't feel as though they are under constant scrutiny, but it is very fair to set up individual conferences with employees to discuss their progress. It is also quite reasonable for employees to realize that you are very interested in their daily work. You are actually doing yourself and them a favor. People want feedback, too. They want to know whether or not they are fulfilling the vision. These scheduled conference sessions should be private. Allow the employee to discuss the findings with other employees if he or she wants to, but you are giving them the opportunity to keep this private. You owe them that courtesy.

Employee appreciation

Have you hired a real winner or winners? I certainly hope so, and you want to keep them. The Raving Fans should be your clients, but they should also

1. In keeping with the Raving Fan concept, let's reward the employee with $100 and a paid day off when he or she gets a referral letter from a client, due to that referral letter was referred a new prospect , and had a phone conference with that referral source. That is really keeping everyone happy.

2. Host a surprise lunch for an employee you know has worked especially hard on a project.

3. Offer professional development or seminars for highly-motivated individuals and pay their way.

4. Buy season tickets to a favorite team and raffle those off at a team meeting.

5. Remember birthdays and get-well wishes for the individual and their families.

7. Have your employees choose a social chairman to plan some fun events outside of the office. Keep the events simple.

8. A recent nation-wide study showed that employees value praise and money as equal motivators! How many times have we missed the opportunity to tell an employee that he or she did a great job on a project?

9. Offer an employee more challenging work. This sends the message that they are respected and valued. This should be done with promotion in mind, when possible.

10. Choose a team leader or a motivated individual to mentor others. This is a great ego boost.

11. Give the gift of time and offer a productive worker a day or a half day off to have fun. Use the feedback ideas or suggestions that your employees have given you. Don't let that well of ideas go dry!

12. Plan on extending a holiday (usually Christmas) treat such as a luncheon or dinner to your staff. They will thank you!

These are some ideas. Try asking your employees for more. People are very clever and come up with great suggestions. One office I heard about had a "Reward Bowl." They had taken a conventional fish bowl and told the employees to come up with one tangible and realistic award for their peers. The staff loved it. Everyone was involved in an enjoyable project.

Balance of perspective

Having a balance of what's good for the team as a whole, and for the individual is important. Everyone will have a tendency to view situations from their own perspective, view point, personality, and experience. It is the responsibility of those in leadership and/or those who own the company to consider all perspectives.

The tendency of employees will often be to view things personally and what's best for them as will also be the perspective for owners as well. The difference in most situations is that the owner will normally continue to be there after many of those employees will have gone onto other positions. To really obtain the best balanced perspective it's ideal to have everyone on the team fully committed to the long-term. If all parties are committed to the long-term success it will tend to force individuals into a more bigger picture perspective of what's best for everyone over the long-term, rather than a more short-termed perspective, which we can all fall into that type of thinking.

If a company is losing money and the team as a whole is taking responsibility for the loses that's a great sign of a mature team. When companies are making a profit everyone is willing to share with others as to why they are a large part of the reason as to why there is a profit. When there are losses is what really tests owners, leaders, and team members as to who will take responsibility, what they are willing to do about it, how much they have at risk or are wiling to risk will really show how is in the best position to make the best choices for the company as a whole.

Anything leadership can do to help people grow and take more personal responsibility for the outcome, both profit and losses, will help the team to mature and be stronger. As individuals take more personal ownership the overall strength of the team will grow and provide the owner's with more freedom.

Conclusion

This chapter can truly be the most enjoyable to carry out. It is really a time for the leader to show what he or she is made of to the company. The leadership of a company is paramount to its success. Leaders who reinforce the vision they have so carefully crafted give everyone direction that is productive. Leaders who are willing to ask for feedback from clients and employees exemplify an open approach that is rewarded over and over. People respond to leaders who are willing to listen and learn. Leaders who make employee appreciation an integral part of the operation score many points. Basically we all know that working is part of why we are here, but how much better to know that the work you do is appreciated? It makes "I *get* to do this job" really true.

Chapter 9 – MEETING

"As any jazz musician knows, it takes flexibility and adaptability for improvisation to create beauty." - Doc Children and Bruce Crier in *From Chaos to Coherence*

A.   How often should you meet?

B.   How to get the most out of the hour meeting

C.   Action items at the end of every meeting

How often should you meet?

Obviously a good leader realizes that keeping the team at task is a primary goal. It is wise to plan meetings for your employees that will help to reinforce the goals and the vision of the company. My experience has shown that these meetings can be beneficial on many levels.

1.   They give the leader a chance to re-evaluate the company's current progress.

2.   They allow the employees to express their concerns and accomplishments.

3.   They foster cooperation between team members who can be informed of the other member's issues.

An effective leader is open to constant re-evaluations of his or her company. Does that mean changing the direction of the company weekly or monthly? NO! But it does mean that the leader is open to listening to the department heads as they explain the week's workload. Since the leader is best positioned to keep the ship sailing in one main direction, he or she must be ready with suggestions and ideas to assist the members. This should not be thought of as a scolding session or a time to put the employees on the carpet, but rather an opportunity to problem solve. I don't want to make this sound easier than it really is because that couldn't be farther from the truth. A real leader knows that meetings can make or break relationships within his or her company.

There are a few suggestions that I have learned. Some of these have been learned the hard way and have cost me the support of some productive people. It is extremely important to prepare for that meeting like a coach facing a challenging team. Why? Your employees are, for the most part, trying to carry out the wishes of your company. They know the rules and the vision. However, they are about to come to a meeting with some genuine concerns. You, the head coach, have to be prepared to discuss those concerns without being judgmental. It is a tricky line to walk. It has been my experience that most employees will tell you that they generally enjoy their job. After all, they applied for it, trained for it, and participated in it. Yet, a tension-filled weekly meeting can set a tone that sends normally content people back to their desks with some pretty bad vibes. The leader has to get a handle on those feelings before the meeting ends.

a. Allow your employees to add items to the agenda that concern them directly

b. Keep a clock handy and contain your (leader's) remarks to only about 10 minutes of the meeting.

c. Keep that clock ticking and make sure that other members don't monopolize the meeting.

d. Be sure to end the meeting on a positive note that sends people back with a clear goal for the next week.

I have found that giving the employees a chance to be a part of the agenda is really effective. That is not giving up control; it is merely acknowledging

the fact that the employees have real issues that need to be addressed. How can this best be accomplished? In today's world, I find that sending out my agenda via e-mail three days before the meeting is wise, and I then tell my employees to add any items they feel are important. Since we all have time constraints, I try to keep the entire agenda to no more than ten items – including the ideas from the staff. Have you ever walked into a meeting and been handed an agenda with 30 or more points on it? Was your first reaction to leave the building? I think anyone would feel that way. Obviously, the concerns of others will never be addressed. There is no time! Keep it short and simple. Remember, these meetings are a regular part of the company.

Since most leaders will feel the need to begin the meeting with their comments, it is wise to keep a clock close by. Today's world is controlled by time, and your employees are obviously thinking about the work that awaits them after the meeting. Get to the point of the meeting in a pleasant manner and let the agenda begin. Too often a leader comes to a meeting with other concerns or a recent call that affects the company and somehow that becomes the focus of the meeting. This should not be the case. There is a technique that I think will help you in this situation. Try the mindset of compartmentalizing. This is simply a system that tells one to stay on the topic at hand. Some of us struggle more with this than others. If circumstances rule your life, it will be more difficult to enter a meeting with a clear head for the agenda. I do feel that you have to do your best to let the "circumstances" of everyday living take a break while you give your employees your undivided attention. Keep in mind that you can't hear about ALL their trials and tribulations. Stay focused. The ten-minute rule is a good one and people's attention spans will thank you for that time frame. Also, it sends the clear message that you will devote time to their concerns.

Now, the next point can be as tricky because some team leaders, particularly the driver and expressive personalities, will want you to spend more time on their agenda point. This is just not fair to the others. Think about how interesting this can get with four or five "leaders" in on your team meeting. I am again reminded of the sixteen type-A personalities who compete on the *Apprentice* TV show. No wonder the sparks fly – everyone is a born leader. Your job as the facilitator is to keep this strong group focused. They totally deserve the time to discuss their issues, but no one person should control the entire meeting. As you know, this will become evident very quickly and others will resent it.

This is a clear-cut method to lead by example. You build fairness into your company. If you care about keeping your employees focused on the company's vision, you have to allow direct input. Be assured that a leader who really promotes fairness will be rewarded, but the path to fairness is often difficult. Let me give you an example.

At any point in time a firm can be struggling with finances. Often this means that clients have not paid their bills or expected business has not come through. Obviously the leader is keenly aware of this situation. Since the best interests of the company are paramount to this individual, he or she finds it really difficult to not let the financial woes color everything that happens. Now picture a meeting with department heads who are coming in with their individual concerns. What are they greeted with? A leader who hits them with the bad news of low revenue is waiting at the door. Does it ruin the meeting? Yes! Everyone is suddenly concerned with their future in the company. Instead of focusing on problem-solving techniques, the team is focusing on the next paycheck. How can a leader avoid this doom and gloom scenario?

I would suggest a totally different meeting approach at this time. Allow the department heads to start with their agenda points. Give them the opportunity to air the pluses and minuses of the week. This sends the message that their issues are important to the operation of the firm. As you near closure at the end of the hour, this is the time when the reality of the company has to be addressed. If you had planned to leave on a totally positive note, this may not be the week. However, you can avoid the "sinking ship" feeling if you are honest and supportive. You want to send them back to work with a plan to solve the problem. Enlist their help, don't send them spiraling down into a hole. The approach makes all the difference. Trust me, the team method is never more important than when the financial sheet looks grim. Rally the team and see the results happen. Scare tactics seldom work; concrete ways to tackle the problem gives people hope and direction. Again, lead by example!

How to get the most out of the hour meeting

I know that most of my readers, if not all, have been involved in hour-long meetings that seem to fly by and other meetings that seemingly take hours to complete. I am very familiar with the meetings where employees are seen doodling, working on other projects, looking at their watches, or filling out a resume – hopefully not that bad. One has to remember that this is a block of time that is being given up by all. The assumption is that everyone has work to do. This should enhance the company and give people direction, not waste their time and the time of the leader.

Following the 10-minute rule for discussion of agenda items is really a great way to stay on the topic. I have spoken with many people who give seminars and are in a teaching capacity. It is wise to remember that most people are rather trained by today's fast society. Whether we like it or not, most people are ready for a new topic in an hour-long meeting. They are smart enough to realize that they will have to return to their desks and ponder the suggestions from their own agenda point and the thoughts of others; however, it is wise to move on so that others can feel a part of the process. Haven't we all been at the doctor's office and waited for a long period of time? If you are already sick, you are suddenly getting sicker as you anticipate a waiting time that is much too long. The same principle applies to a meeting. All the people need to be heard in a reasonable amount of time.

Another suggestion that can work is being willing to relocate for the team meeting. Some leaders find that an occasional meeting at a restaurant, perhaps for breakfast, can be effective. This sounds enjoyable on the surface because workers are always looking for a change of venue. As the leader, you have to judge whether or not this is productive. Again, you need to lead by example and set the right tone. If these restaurant meetings are the norm, people will get down to business and enjoy the atmosphere. If you don't do these very often, or choose a loud location, you may find yourself wondering how this is helping the company's cause. Obviously, bringing some treats directly to the office is another suggestion. This can be a shared responsibility. Most people are very willing to be a part of a meeting that asks the members to share. This gives everyone a chance to participate.

In summation, I can't emphasize enough the importance of an agenda that addresses the needs of the people at the meeting. The leader has to prepare this ahead of time so that the team is given the opportunity to discuss their issues and problem solve with others. We have all been to meetings where a leader "flies" in with no game plan, and the meeting's direction takes off in a million tangents. This is not productive for anyone.

Action items at the end of the meeting

I truly believe that this is the area that can give the most direction for the team members. However, I would caution against just handing out "action items" before some closure is accomplished. For instance, let's assume that a team member comes to the meeting with a viable concern about a client who is really unhappy with the services provided. The team member has spent hours trying to find a more agreeable plan for the client via e-mails, phone calls, and mailings.

The member has spoken to others about the situation and is literally at the end of the trail for ways to keep this client happy. What to do? Obviously, the member has put this concern down as an agenda point. Now we have come to the end of the meeting. Ideally, the member has been given some great suggestions to reach out to the client, but, if the problem seems really a bit overwhelming, it might not be in everyone's best interest to load that person down with twenty action items for the next week. You have to really "read" the atmosphere in the meeting and know when to hand out the action items and when to focus on the issues at hand.

A teacher I know told me that this is a cardinal rule in classroom management. There are wonderful teaching moments that come along and make the profession all it should be. There are also lessons that overwhelm students and leave them audibly groaning. The teacher has to know how to close those lessons. If over half of the group is genuinely scratching their heads in dismay, this isn't the time to hand out that term paper assignment that is due in a few weeks. Common sense would tell you to address the problem at hand. A good leader feels this as the meeting progresses. One might need to meet privately with the individual who is having so much difficulty and send the others back to productive work. Your goal as the leader is to emulate the vision and give hope and possibility out to the employees. Don't lose sight of that purpose!

I do want to give you some good ideas for some typical action items that do set a positive tone for your company. These are rather tried and true and generally give people direction without overwhelming their already full work load.

1. Let's come back next week and relate one positive way we helped a client or a team member.

2. Let's come back next week with one way we found to be more efficient at our job.

3. Let's come back next week with an example of how the company's vision worked for us.

These are all ways to keep the focus on a company that is endeavoring to make a profit without constant involvement. These three things give people ideas to make their work easier and more productive. They are designed to pull the troops together and send them out with a more efficient way to operate.

Conclusion

Meetings are critical to the success of a company. Don't underestimate the impact. Many leaders have lost support because of that. Be aware of the tendency to have too many meetings. It wears people out. Having a meeting once a week would be a good rule of thumb. Keep that agenda handy and be fair about time others are allowed to share. The action items are important, but the paramount focus should be on sending the employees back to work with a positive and productive attitude. "Read" your meeting atmosphere and strive to get the most out of everyone by being fair and encouraging. Those methods are proven winners.

Chapter 10 - RUNNING (HANDING IT OFF TO OTHERS)

Sara Paddison: HIDDEN POWER OF THE HEART "Surrender does not diminish our power, it enhances it."

A.   Managing from a distance
B.   Reporting – how to assess people's progress
C.   Using numbers and percentages to motivate and manage

Managing from a distance

The overall goal of this book has been to give you practical ways to manage a business that is profitable without the owner's constant supervision. This requires that the business professional put all the aforementioned systems into place efficiently and train his staff to use the systems properly. So much of what I have shared with you is possible because those systems are customized to the client and the staff really knows how to engineer the program. It is fair to say that there is really no other way to have true peace of mind than to know that you are working with good systems and good people to carry them out. The preparation for all this has been explained in past chapters and it is critical to success.

I do meet regularly with my staff, as explained, and I often say, "Please take me out of the picture as you care for our clients." This can be a bit scary at first, but essentially it is fundamental to my overall purpose. I want my staff to feel confident and ready to leave me out of the process as they keep the systems working. I will be honest, there is a tendency on the part of my staff to bring me back into the picture. It is with time and effort that they truly feel that they have the power to make it all happen. A business owner and the team must have the understanding that initially no one will probably provide the level of servicing that the owner/founder can. We often end up going backwards to move forward. The owner must understand that, over the long-term, they can not provide anything close to the level of service that a strong team can provide. Allow challenges in the short-term to gain the strength in the long-term.

I have included the following system that I regularly use to help my staff find out where we stand with the clients. This is really a helpful tool because it enables the staff to assess the client's satisfaction regarding our products and services. It is meant to be an open and honest survey of the customer's real feelings about the service he or she is receiving. The staff is trained to become familiar with it and use it to continue to customize the needs and desires of the client. I have endeavored to keep it simple and forthright. We all know how busy everyone is, but it is important to get a reading of their satisfaction. By having my staff use this tool, I am essentially allowing them to get a true picture of the client's needs. The staff member can then come to a meeting with the necessary information to reach the client on a consistent basis. This allows me to manage from a distance because I don't have to be directly involved in all the systems that my client's benefit from. We are currently working on moving this whole system to a turnkey Internet-based system which will make it more effective, cost less, and provide an easier way for the client to provide feedback.

1. On a 1-to-10 scale with 10 being the best, please rate the following:

               ___ a. Overall service from the company

               ___ b. Ease of use of the product

___ c. Quality of training and how well you understood the product

___ d. How effectively you used the product

___ e. How consistently you followed through using the product/service to its full potential

___ f. Getting a GREAT return on your investment

___ g. Effectiveness of the product

___ h. How hard our team worked to make your experience a positive on

___ i. Creating a WOW experience for you

___ j. Overall satisfaction with your investment into the product or service

2. What was the most positive aspect of your experience, and would you be willing to recommend this product to someone else?

3. If you could make one suggestion as to how _____ (the product and/or service) could be improved, what would that suggestion be?

4. Is there anything up to this point that might cause you to think you may not continue to use the product or service in the long-term development of your business and career?   What would be one suggestion on how we could overcome this potential challenge?

5. Do you have any other comments, suggestions, ideas, or input that you would

like to share with our team on what we could do to assist you?

Once the staff member has been given the above information, they are prepared to better serve the client. Since the staff has been so well trained, they can make sure the systems fit the client. Also, this frees me up to focus on the larger issues of the firm. The company is making a profit without me because I have trained my people to assess the clients on a regular basis and bring these concerns to our meetings. At that point, we can efficiently work together to solve the problems that arise.

Reporting – how to assess people's progress

We have put systems into place that give all parties – client and staff – a quick and thorough assessment of how the tools are working. A percentage system is in place so that the client can readily determine how well the tools are really functioning. Our basic plan is to increase our client's business by 25 to 50%. We want to measure that goal and see if it is happening for our client. In addition, we want to be able to give the client a real reduction in his or her work time of ten to fifteen hours per week. The optimum situation is to increase business and decrease hours worked. This will not happen overnight, but we have systems in place to measure that goal.

I have included our full program benefits. This is to give you an idea of how comprehensive these tools are. We are striving to make our client's life and business run more smoothly, so we offer a full package to do that. These tools offer a complete and thorough program for companies who wish to use them. Years of effort have gone into these tools, but once they are established, the leader can manage from a distance with a staff that has been properly trained to implement the necessary tools. Every tool, process, and system we offer to our clients we use ourselves. We know these systems work. Every business needs tools, processes, and systems. With the right business plan, advisors, and people on the team you can turn almost any system you have developed for your own business as something you can offer to your clients, referral sources, vendors, etc. something of added value which will help their business to make a profit without them. By helping them you will grow your business as well.

Some of the programs/systems include:

- ◆ Development of a detailed twelve-month business plan.

- ◆ Business consulting and coaching.

- ◆ Advanced training in personality assessment and sales development.

- ◆ Turnkey relationship marketing.

- ◆ Advanced business development training.

- ◆ Time, activity, and productivity tracking and training.

- ◆ Business development seminars and follow-up.

- ◆ Training on how to open new referral sources.

- ◆ Tools to build loyalty with each of your referral sources.

- ◆ Turnkey technology systems and solutions.

- ◆ Multi-media to reproduce key sales functions, service functions, and training.

- ◆ On-line tools, systems, and information to assist clients by growing personally and professionally.

- ◆ Custom programming to meet specific business needs to maximize overall effectiveness.

- ◆ Turnkey on-line culture development systems with ability to customize.

I have found that the clients who implement all of these components receive the largest benefits. Every new system we develop we ask for input from our clients, so once these systems, tools, and processes are proven we're able to offer them to each of our clients, referral sources, vendors grow their businesses. Again, the more we can assist those we touch on a daily basis the greater our success will be as a team. We obviously keep in touch with our clients on a monthly basis by phone. At that time we emphasize the core actions that will make a difference in their profits

My observations have shown me that a client who conscientiously carries out the above plan can and will see results that are measurable. We literally keep a tally sheet for the client using a point value to show him or her just how many of the actions are being implemented on a regular basis. I don't want to reduce this to just a simple concept, but let's think of a typical Christmas list for the family. Have you checked off all of the family members so that no one is disappointed on Christmas morning? Consistency is essential. This is the primary purpose. Leave no stone unturned when using this plan. When we show the client areas that have been neglected, they readily see target areas that need work. I am sure we can all identify with the visual black and white format of seeing where we need direction. After all these years in the business, it is still evident to me that people need to SEE what they are and are not doing. We all think we have checked off the present list, but somehow something is missing as we begin to open the gifts. How did this happen? You want to take that mystery out of the picture. By offering an action check list, you are giving the client a clear and simple way to determine his effort in this endeavor.

Let's assume we have checked off all the action points. Don't we now have a committed client who is following directions exactly? Are we not proud of our coaching skills? Didn't we promise our client an efficient plan with tools that really work? However, just like all those push-ups at the gym, there has to be a reason for the effort. If a profit is to be attained without a lot of supervision, the client has to know why these actions matter. What do they accomplish? Are we just enforcing discipline for the sake of discipline? That only works for a short time.

Here's the payoff: the checklist of necessary actions will bring in the continued business that your client so desperately desires. It is human nature to focus on the finished product – the slim body in the mirror after all those push-ups. Yet, we all know that won't last without the proper upkeep. Your systems provide that upkeep. The discipline isn't just for the sake of discipline – it keeps the wheels of business turning. The ultimate goal is continued business! When your client sees the new business coming in because of these systems, he will realize that the profits are continual.

I suppose I have to be fair and address the stubborn client. Just imagine putting all these systems in place and having a client who expects miracles without lifting a finger. I always wondered where the client got that idea, but it does happen. How do you motivate that person effectively? I find that results often speak much louder than words. When this unwilling client sees that he or she is basically sitting on the bench during the game, it brings it all into focus. That is when your team really needs to brainstorm ways to reach out to that client. Some people get the results back and spring into action; others go into denial, and some resent the wake-up call. I would strongly suggest that you and your team reflect on the personality types that you have gathered from the client. Reach that person is his or her best place. People will modify their behavior if you find the way to send the message.

The team is well trained in the four personality types, and they are the ones who have been so directly involved with the clients. Allow them to reach out to these individuals and devise a plan to create action and then results. The systems will scientifically measure your results. The results a client sees are directly correlated to their effort. If he or she completes 90% of the plan, they will see 90% of the results they want. I have found that relating those statistics to people, regardless of their personality type, gets the same result. The numbers do not lie. The visual presentation of their program and whether or not they have fulfilled the requirements speaks for itself. Once again, the goal of making a profit without constant input is accomplished. I let the checklist guide the client. People don't respond well to lectures, but when they see numbers, it makes a difference.

Ideally, you would have a leadership team of at least three people who you really trust and have proven themselves to have strong value, that are hard workers, and who are loyal. Of those three individuals, it would be ideal if the new president were one of those three and everyone on the team agreed that that person was the best to take over. If your company is not there at this point, there is great risk in handing over the authority to someone who is not proven within your company. In the selection process for a president to replace myself at Synergy we developed the following list and rated each person being considered on the following items:

Rate 1 to 10 with 10 being the best for each of the following:

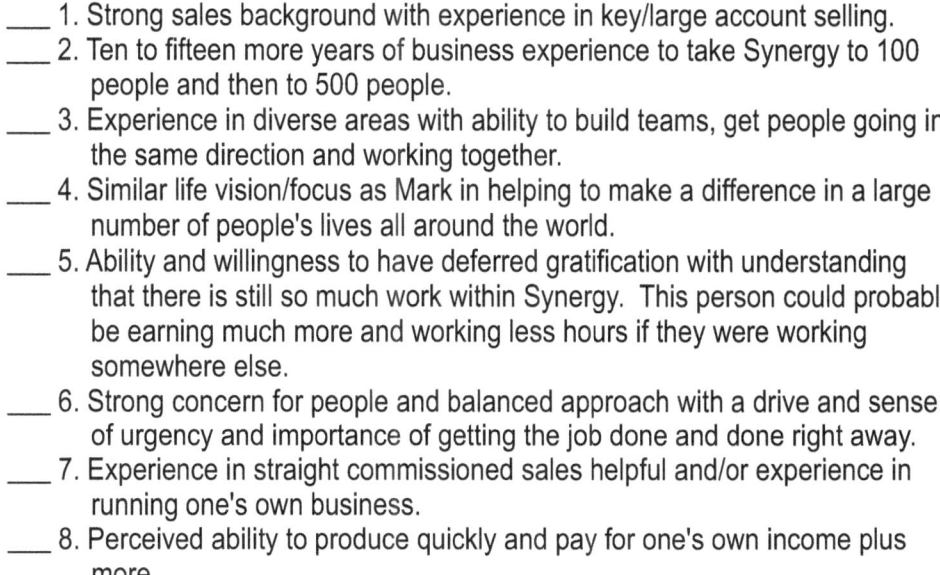

___ 1. Strong sales background with experience in key/large account selling.
___ 2. Ten to fifteen more years of business experience to take Synergy to 100 people and then to 500 people.
___ 3. Experience in diverse areas with ability to build teams, get people going in the same direction and working together.
___ 4. Similar life vision/focus as Mark in helping to make a difference in a large number of people's lives all around the world.
___ 5. Ability and willingness to have deferred gratification with understanding that there is still so much work within Synergy. This person could probably be earning much more and working less hours if they were working somewhere else.
___ 6. Strong concern for people and balanced approach with a drive and sense of urgency and importance of getting the job done and done right away.
___ 7. Experience in straight commissioned sales helpful and/or experience in running one's own business.
___ 8. Perceived ability to produce quickly and pay for one's own income plus more.

Book Conclusion

It is my sincerest wish that you walk away from reading this book with concrete ways to achieve a profit for your business. When business people choose to read literature about their profession, I have found that they tend to be truly motivated people. Unfortunately, the poor soul who is trying to keep his business afloat seldom has time for professional reading. However, it is safe to say that practical methods to efficiently run a business can benefit any and all professionals. In my estimation, the team approach I have implemented in my business has been its greatest asset. I can't emphasize enough the importance of hiring the right people who share your vision and passion and who are very comfortable with the systems you have in place. When I do coaching for clients, I stress the importance of getting the right people in the right job. No progress is possible if the team isn't behind the project. When you have these systems in place, you will enjoy the reward of watching a business grow and you won't be managing every detail. Now that is a true reward!

Quotes:

Introduction - Oliver Wendell Holmes: "Man's mind once stretched by a new idea, never regains its original dimension."

1. Valuing – Bidpai "Honest men esteem and value nothing so much in the world as a real friend."

2. Questioning – Ella Wheeler Wilcox (1850 - 1919) "No question is ever settled until it is settled right. Settle the question right."

3. Trusting – Laurence Sterne (1730 - 1768) "Trust that man in nothing who has not a conscience in everything."

4. Solving – Richard Bach "Every problem has a gift for you in its hands."

5. Coaching – Vincent Van Gogh – "How can I be useful, of what service can I be? "

6. Hiring – Luke 10:7 (New Testament) – "The laborer is worthy of his hire."

7. Training – Mark Twain - "There is nothing training cannot do. Nothing is above its reach. It can turn bad morals to good; destroy bad principles and recreate good ones; it can lift men to angelship."

8. Leading – Robert K. Greenleaf – "The only test of leadership is that somebody follows."

9. Meeting – Doc Children and Bruce Crier FROM CHAOS TO COHERENCE – "As any jazz musician knows, it takes flexibility and adaptability for improvisation to create beauty.

10. Running - Sara Paddison – Hidden Power of the Heart – "Surrender does not diminish our power, it enhances it."

Stretching can be beneficial on many levels. Physically, we generally feel better when we stretch our bodies. Emotionally, we gain new insights that we might never have known because we stretch ourselves to see all the perspectives that others may have. Spiritually, we enhance our faith as we see life situations work out because we were willing to stretch and trust. These are large concepts that are literally life-long desires for most people. We expect to spend a great deal of time learning how to stretch and accept new ways of enriching our lives. Isn't it reasonable to assume that we will also stretch in our careers? Can we be open to new ideas and methods to make the stretching more profitable? That is what this book is all about.

I have owned my own businesses since 1974. Some of those years have been spent working for others. When I first left college, I thought that was a stretch because I had to mold my learning with the goals and plans of my employer. Obviously, my three degrees in business couldn't have totally prepared me for the real world. Nothing beats real experience. Sometimes I felt as though the stretching was really over the top. After marriage to my college sweetheart and the start of our family, I quickly realized that providing for my family was a definite priority. Many of the individuals reading this book can identify with the feeling that the real world asks more of us on a daily basis than we often feel prepared to deliver. That is why I wrote this book. I wanted to share some of my most practical ways to help others in business. You may view this book and its ideas as a stretch, but I guarantee you that you will look at your own business in a new light and it will give you new ideas to make it work.

Frankly, it has taken decades to develop these ideas and systems and I have hundreds of people to thank for their investment into my life. I am sure that many of you feel as though you have spent more than enough years trying to make your business profitable. Why are the profits and feelings of personal fulfillment not what you expected? Why do you find yourself so involved in every decision? Why does the typical forty-hour week seem laughable because you are spending so much more time on your business? These are honest questions that most business people struggle with on a daily basis. I have been in your situation, and I can identify with the pain of not reaping what you are trying to diligently to sow.

It is my hope that you will be open to the new ideas that are presented in this book. Perhaps you will read a chapter and think that the basic concept is really quite fundamental. Maybe you will think back to people in your life who have tried to send you the same message. Yet, you realize that now is the time to focus on your business and how it can make a profit without you. Some of you will be thinking that it isn't making much of a profit WITH YOU. That is why this book is invaluable to you. Your desire to stretch and become a better business person is why this book appeals to you. I am about to offer you ways to make your business thrive. Imagine a business that succeeds when you put the right systems in place. Be open to new ideas that can change the direction of your business.